MY BOOK OF MIGHTY MANTRAS

A Daily Dose of
Love, Wisdom, and Mindfulness
A Daily Reminder of our
Power, Purpose, and Potential

Book 1 of the **My Mini Books Series**™

Written by
Donna Martini

My Mini Book of Might Mantras
Copyright: © 2018 by Donna Martini
All rights reserved by the author,
Donna Martini and publisher
DM Enterprises, LLC

MyMantraMouse.com
My Mini Book of Mighty Mantras is Book 1 in a series of
My Mini Books™
MantraMouse® is a trademarked character.
All rights reserved by
Donna Martini
DM Enterprises, LLC

ISBN: 978-0-998-0392-0-6

Cover and MantraMouse™ Cartoon
Creator and Illustrator:
Donna Martini

Illustration and Graphic Artistry:
Cheryl Edwards
William Horne
Lisa Michaels
Lauren Pastor

Copy Editing:
Donna Martini

Format Consultant:
Jessica Leiser

Content Readers:
Rene Fiechter
Neil McKenna
Garrick Turano

This book is dedicated in loving memory to
my friend and graphic artist,

Cheryl Capella Edwards

*Cheryl, my muse and constant source of inspiration
for so many years, you brought all my drawings,
creations, and imaginings into being; you brought
MantraMouse to life! The body that housed your Soul
may be gone, but I refuse to let our relationship go with
it. Know that your beautiful spirit lives on; it fills my
room with your talent while I design and allows your
encouraging words to echo in my head. We will forever
be creating amazing things together!*

*With love and so much gratitude for your contribution
to my life and work…*

Until we meet again, D.

Contents

Medical Disclaimer: *Do not rely solely on the information in this book or use it as an alternative to medical advice from your doctor or other professional healthcare providers. Please acknowledge that because of the nature of a book, there is a limited ability to communicate full concepts, and some information shared might be incomplete and misleading for your specific condition or circumstances. The author can't possibly know each of her reader's immediate needs. Her story of healing from Crohn's Disease should in no way be considered professional medical advice about how you should treat your condition or any disorder you may have. You should never delay seeking or disregard professional advice, nor should you discontinue medical treatment because of information you read in these pages. This book was written to help readers achieve a new perspective on their own physical, emotional, mental, and spiritual potential to help themselves. It was the author's intention to share her research about meditation, mindfulness, and prayer and to offer a broader view that will lead readers to research and explore additional healing modalities that can help them on their unique journey. She wishes to make no claim that mantras are a cure and that repeating them should wholly replace medical or psychiatric treatment. She wishes, instead, to help her readers take more control of their minds, bodies, and lives, and to enhance their ability to remain as positive, focused, mindful, powerful, and spiritually connected as they can be. This book is about the inner journey that affects the outer journey; it is about the power of faith, compassion, forgiveness, goodness, and most especially, love.* ♥

"Be faithful in small things because it is in them that your strength lies."
Mother Teresa

"Spreading some goodness today."

Introduction
A Note from Me to You

Dear *Fellow Journeyer,*

     Through a lifetime's worth of trials, I have learned many ways to lift my spirit, to heal from illness and trauma, and to overcome sorrow, depression, and emotional pain. I endured physical, sexual, and mental abuse that led to ultimate forgiveness and eventually, restoration of my psyche and persona. I have risen from brokenness, disease, and near death, to healing and amazing spiritual and personal growth. It is my belief that my ability to persevere came from prayer, mindfulness, and an innate process I discovered within myself I call *Positive Manipulation*®. The writings contained herein are an accumulation of the very mindsets I used on the road to wellness, which makes me a firsthand witness to some of what we as humans are capable of achieving. *I want to share all of this with you.* Before I do that, though, allow me to explain why I believe my life experience can help you.

     Helping myself and others go from survival to 'thrival' has afforded me an education in humility, unconditional love and forgiveness, energy manipulation, and what I consider Soul-to-Soul Communication. Although no school teaches these life skills, and there is no diploma issued after trial and triumph, there is wisdom gained and a degree of skillfulness that is achieved. More importantly, there is a spiritual payoff—an awareness that we are never alone. Something far greater than our human minds can comprehend exists for our benefit and is always willing to grace us with wisdom, strength, and fortitude. I began to receive all three of these virtues (in the form of guidance and information that seemed to come directly into my right ear) in the early 1990s while going through my divorce. At first, I thought I was getting smarter; I even took an IQ test! When the results showed no significant increase since high school, I had to ask where the wisdom was coming from and why—why was I able to triumph so steadfastly during this emotional challenge but others in the past, not so much? Was it because the stakes were so high? Did the degree of difficulty in the challenge make the difference, or was it my degree of commitment to overcome it?

Most people will admit that it took facing a difficult life episode to help them realize their own potential, and that makes sense to me. When my dog MyLove was only six months old, my daughter Heather and I took her to the beach to play. There were many other dogs there, and MyLove was thrilled to engage with them. But when a Labrador Retriever she was playing with ran into the water, MyLove ran in after him. Heather and I panicked because MyLove is a mystery of mixed breeds, and we didn't know if she could swim. Turns out, neither did she! As soon as her paws could no longer touch the harbor's sandy floor, she did an immediate about face and started hightailing it back to the beach. In her race to get to shore and return to safety, she started paddling furiously, and that's when it happened… She realized she was supported by the water and in full control of where she wanted to go. In an instant, she overcame her fear and did another one-eighty, heading right back out to join her new friend. It was a 'pivotal' moment of triumph and surprise for all of us that really stoked a fire in me. I wondered, if life-altering self-discovery can be realized in a single moment of fear, what other innate abilities do we have that we don't know we have?

Looking back on my own ability to rise from adversity, I have to admit that fear and extreme discomfort were necessary precursors for my spiritual growth and positive, forward movement. Without both, I might have stayed in denial and my as-is condition, never knowing what I was capable of achieving. All too often, many of us have to get fed up, too tired, or too desperate and afraid before we will move from where we are. On the flip side, I have also witnessed many people achieve greatness without needing adverse conditions to prompt certain accomplishments. Just like MyLove, they held some fear but were still motivated by passion and desire. When I juxtaposed these scenarios—rising *from* adversity and rising *for* a desired outcome—the answer seemed simple: We don't have to wait to be pushed and then hope the power to overcome will be magically *released*. We can, instead, willfully ask for it daily, and allow for our innate potential to be continually *unleashed*.

From what I have witnessed, we all possess amazing spiritual 'lift' and when we choose to rise, we rise! When we decide to be our best, do our best, and strive for the best outcome we can achieve, we flourish. It is those goals that create a shift that allows our soulful selves—not our human selves—to be our driving force. It is then that we acquire so much more than our education to rely on; more than our past to define us; more than just our body and mind to take us where we want to go. We are, at that moment and every moment thereafter, at our most powerful state of being and in our most loving state of awareness, connected to more of the love and power that exists around us. In fact, once we set our intention to do better today than we did yesterday, it becomes almost impossible to stay grounded in a simply human condition. And this, my fellow journeyer, is when we can utilize our innate gifts and all the possibilities that exist in each moment. Because realistically, *we are all, each and every one of us, every single day, always just one decision away from our greatest potential.* And I am so excited to explore that potential with you as we venture on this road to wellness together!

With Love and Light, ⊃.

P.S. Please accept my apology if my choice of names, words, and descriptions contradict your sensibility or religious and spiritual beliefs. *My intention is to honor you, your beliefs, and your life journey.* Anything seemingly contrary is unintentional! My hope is threefold: Firstly, that you will understand the delicate challenge I undertook putting forth information about the most intricate and personal aspects of our spiritual lives. Secondly, that you remain open-minded and open-hearted to receive the love and respect I wrote this book with. Lastly, that the messages and mantras are perceived as all-embracing, meaning they are based on human life principles that revolve around love and goodness and can segue into all theologies without being perceived as spiritually arrogant or in opposition to any religious doctrine or teaching. My ultimate goal is to acknowledge what we all have in common, irrespective of our nationality, race, religion, and education. So thank you for any consideration and tolerance you offer and for sharing your time with me! ♥

PART I

Defining Positive Manipulation®
(PM)

Before I explain PM (Positive Manipulation®), I want to ask you not get hung up on the word *manipulation*. After all, if I gave you a lump of clay and asked you to manipulate it into the shape of a bowl, you wouldn't hesitate to start molding the clay, nor would you question the word, would you? In most dictionaries, the first definition of manipulation is *"to handle or control as if using a tool or mechanism in a skillful manner."* That is the meaning I am referring to and what I'm suggesting we do to any aspect of ourselves that is creating an imbalance or keeping us from reaching our goals. The fact is we are already allowing ourselves to be 'negatively' manipulated by many aspects of our inside and outside worlds. This does not have to continue. We can hear and see differently; we can change our thoughts, emotions, bodies, cells, and energy, which will change our future, the past, our relationships, and all other aspects of our lives. That is what PM is: *The willful act of physically, mentally, and emotionally manipulating what is not working on our behalf into the most appropriate and productive outcome we can achieve.* We do this so we can stay as spiritually driven as our human form will allow.

One day, it just dawned on me...

In an effort to stay loving and forgiving toward my future ex-husband during our separation, I had to talk myself out of some very angry mental and verbal dialogue. I realized I was actually manipulating myself every time I had to interact with him. Honestly, part of me wanted to stay angry. Anger made me feel brave, and I thought it was helping me stay committed to leaving him. That anger-induced bravado though, it often backfired, and for the sake of our kids, *I wanted to keep our marital vows to love and honor even after the divorce papers were signed*. My real objective was to help all of us come through the divorce stronger, not weaker, and for all our lives to get better, not worse. That meant that I would have to get better; better at being *Me.* So I made the commitment to *think, say, and do all things the loving and forgiving way.* As it turned out, that goal broke down to minute-to-minute decisions that not only afforded me and my family a bearable separation and divorce, something unexpected and miraculous also took place: My body, mind, and heart became what I refer to as *SuperCharged.*

Inner thoughts that were once negative and judgmental changed to positive and loving. The former victim and woe-is-me mentality I had allowed myself to dwell in for so long switched to personal responsibility and empowerment. I became aware that I should stop blaming others for what I thought they did to me and instead look at my own participation in the direction my life was heading. After making my pledge to love, all the drama and trauma that had been twisting my persona since childhood was finally revealed. It showed me how what I went through *back then* was affecting me *right now.* In time, I was led to healing from many aspects of my past, and as healing took place, I was exerting less mental and emotional energy on what happened years ago, because I was happier focusing on the beautiful future I wanted to walk into. There were body changes, too, that came from a new found passion for healthy living, organic cooking, yoga, dance, and Pilates. I spent more time hiking, horseback riding, and gardening; everything that brought me closer to nature. I felt led and guided through my career, which immediately took off and allowed for more money to come in. PM kickstarted a comprehensive wellness journey that fills me daily with love, inspiration, compassion, and gratitude as it makes every step I take lead to more empowerment, healing, and most importantly, tolerance and forgiveness of myself and others.

About initially starting the process... I will admit that in the very beginning, manipulating my words and actions was like pulling my own teeth! I didn't always stay true to my commitment to love, but that became less and less of a challenge after seeing the amazing results that ensued when I did stay committed. The more I used PM, the easier it was to do. The more I used love as my driving force, the more inspiration would flow. It became obvious to me that there were two distinct speakers in my head: One was an astute and influential pathfinder who professed love and always gave the best advice; the other, not so much! They seemed so completely different I decided to name them Big Donna and little donna. Big meant louder, and little meant softer. Back then, I considered the bigger voice to be my very human ego, and the little whisper was my Soul. I'm happy to report that after years of using the

PM process, the voices have flipped. The whisper is now so *mighty*, I find it easier and easier to consistently say *no* to that stubborn ego of mine while saying *yes* to its very loving and altruistic counterpart. This is not just my belief, by the way; this is and has been my real-life experience! And perhaps you are already living this way but if not, this could be what is in store for you.

Energy: The Essence of Life

If you are currently going through an adverse situation and are in need of more abundance or more understanding about your relationship with your spiritual self; if you desire to heal from your past so you can achieve more in your present and future, you may have energetically connected with this book. There is a part of you that is leading, guiding, and bringing you toward all that will help you achieve your life goals, most especially if you attached an unselfish motive to them. The majority of us believe we possess the ability to connect to some kind of higher understanding and ethereal power. Depending, though, on the religious or spiritual philosophy we adopt, that power can come from the creator they call God or a God of another name, such as Yahweh, Jehovah, Allah, Brahman, Krishna, etc. There are those who consider the origin of power to be a non-being, undefined, so they use Universe,

Light, Collective Conscience, and other names. Of course, you have your own belief, but irrespective of the name you and I and everyone else give this power, we are all (those who call themselves atheists, included) still experiencing the same phenomena. We are all equipped with emotional and mental capabilities which far exceed human comprehension; we are all beings of energy who are connected to everything, and we are all, in a word, magnificent!

This might sound like 'New Age' philosophy to some, but truthfully, I don't believe there is anything new about it. The idea that humans are capable of achieving amazing feats is not novel, and there is nothing original about the concept of energy or of being connected to ethereal wisdom. I look at it this way: Gravity existed and was being utilized way before the apple fell on Newton's head… way before anyone understood why we were all stuck to the ground. And it's the same for this power source that has been in existence. Theories and beliefs about creation and Divinity were established centuries before the scientific world and spiritualists began their endeavor to figure everything out. Now, though, with recent discoveries about energy, we may be able to shed some light on our *Light*; meaning our inner power and connectivity to our intuitive selves, to each other, our world, and beyond. These new discoveries don't have to contradict our traditional religious beliefs. On the contrary, bringing science and spirituality together might help us finally explain what used to be unexplainable!

Now we are told that we are not matter, we are energy (which may lend some credence to the *"You are a soul with a body, not a body with a soul"* philosophy). Physically speaking, we (our bodies) are just a bunch of water molecules, and we are surrounded by more of the same. On a molecular level, there is nothing really separating us from one another, not even our skin. And we really are *one with the Earth* when we consider that we're made of the same atoms, cells, elements, minerals, and compounds as the air we breathe, the ground we walk upon, the seas encompassing us, the animals we cohabit with, and the vegetation that seem to grow for our benefit. What does that say about our Creator if you believe in One? What does that say about our universe if you don't?

It tells me that no matter how we think we got here or who or what made us, we were specifically designed to connect and symbiotically commune with everything and everyone surrounding us. In my simplistic mind, I find this connective energy synonymous with spirit, but how do we take advantage of it? Where are all our built-in communication tools, receptors, and sensors, and how do we use them for our highest good? How much power do we really possess—mentally and emotionally—to energetically effect positive change in our minds, bodies, relationships, each other's lives, the environment, and our world?

Conducting Power

Going back to the topic of our varied belief systems... You may give all the power and the glory to God or another Divine Being. Maybe you give spiritual energy, the Earth, and our universe all the credit, or you believe we humans are wholly responsible for generating our own steam. I happen to think a combination of all three is needed, but it would probably be more prudent to acknowledge that we can't properly define with words what we just don't yet understand. Since I have no desire to challenge anyone's reality or religion, nor do I want to offend anyone, least of all *you*, I would like to use these pages to explore the science. And in an effort to make this book more effective to use for people of all faiths and denominations, I leave it to each reader to fill in where the actual science and their faith converge.

Today we have evidence that a web of energy exists between us, inside us, and around us. There is proof that we do share with one another the energy of emotion and thought that emanates from our hearts and minds. There is also data which concurs with what most religions have always known: that prayer (communicating our intentions orally, *heartfully*, and mentally) can achieve miracles! What the fields of science and medicine have discovered recently is so profound it's hard for anyone to deny the existence of an intelligent designer. Spiritualists of today are correlating these discoveries with what is written in the Bible, the Dead Sea Scrolls, the Torah, Koran, Talmud, Tao, Tripitaka, Sutras, Zohar, and other religious texts and noting the incredible synergy. Is it possible that the authors and contributors of these ancient books might have been trying to convey the concepts of energy manipulation through their varied languages and limited understanding of the actual science? This potential energizes me, and there is so much more information to share; but for the purpose of keeping this publication 'mini,' more will be covered in depth in my next book about Positive Manipulation®. In the meantime, what *is* being shared here will hopefully help you come to your own conclusions about the power we all have at our disposal.

Soul-to-Soul Communication

There was an experiment conducted some years ago at a major hospital. Its purpose was to find out if mindful prayer could influence a healing outcome among patients with sepsis (a dangerous internal infection that can lead to death). They separated the study into two groups: those who were prayed for and those who were not. The results: although a small difference in the number of deaths was noted (the prayed-for group was slightly less), a significant healing effect was reported in patients who had prayers spoken on their behalf. These people responded better to treatment, left the hospital faster, and symptoms such as fever and infection didn't last as long, nor were they as severe. This led conductors of the study to conclude that prayer could be a useful treatment for sickness and disease. (See study details here at www.ncbi.nlm.nih.gov/pmc/articles/PMC61047.)

The most astonishing aspect of this entire experiment: the people who were doing the praying were unknowingly involved in "retroactive intercessory prayer," meaning their prayer requests were being recited in the present, but the patients they were praying for were actually sick in the past! They were ailing in that hospital at different times over a span of more than 10 years prior to the prayer sessions and the study. While critics had their doubts about the results, it proved to me what I have instinctively known for years: There is a part of us that is not challenged by the concept of time; we can help affect a positive change in the present, the future, *and* the past. All we need to do to create worthwhile change is hold a positive mental intention and back it up with powerful positive emotion. That generates energy that can radiate and co-mingle beyond our bodies. As I have stated before, we are already doing this—energetically connecting to one another and whatever else exists—irrespective of whether we understand it or do it purposefully; regardless of whether we can name, define, identify, or explain any of it.

*"Be careful how you think; your life is shaped by your thoughts." **Proverbs 4:23***

Science Says

Supposedly, what we see of energy—what is tangible—is only about one percent of what actually exists in our world and universe. Imagine then, what we don't know about the space surrounding us…? For now, though, let's concentrate on what we have figured out, starting with what we are made of. Most of us learned that we are about 60 to 70% water, but as I stated previously, almost all of our molecules (about 97.3%) are said to be water molecules; even our bones are made of them. From what I have gathered, scientists haven't been able to explain why, but my commonsense brain asks, *why not?* Consider what water is to us… We are born in it, we subsist by drinking it, and it is in the air that we breathe. We eat food that grows from it and along with every living thing in the world, we would die without it. We sweat and purge water, make babies in water; we use it to heal, restore, cleanse, and baptize our bodies. Famed researcher Masaru Emoto discovered that water molecules found in nature can respond to human emotion, which makes sense considering *we cry water*! So are water molecules what energetically connect us mentally, emotionally, physically, and spiritually to ourselves, each other, and everything on our planet?

Famed scientist Candace Pert calls them *"molecules of emotion"* and contends that all the cells in our body are responding to what we tell them... whatever state of mind we put ourselves in. Think about how this plays out in our everyday lives... If we wanted to achieve let's say, happiness, we would need to get rid of whatever negative yappiness was going on in our heads. The reason is that we can't reach our desired state of being while we consistently insinuate its opposite. Put another way: we can't keep saying, "I'm miserable, but I want to be happy" and then expect our mood to change! If we cannot mentally create the state of being we desire, how will our cells—which encompass and affect every single nuance of our bodies—know and understand or be in alignment with the state of being we are trying to create?

Consider some other influences that make it difficult to stay focused on what we truly desire... Everyone and everything we are exposed to, ingest, hear, see, touch, live in, and live through can have an influence on our minds, bodies, decisions, and the paths we choose. Some of what we experience leaves such an impact, it changes us genetically without our knowledge. A recent scientific study showed the genetic changes caused by severe trauma in Holocaust victims were actually passed down to their children and grandchildren. The researchers refer to this phenomenon as "epigenetic inheritance," and along with this kind of extreme mental and emotional duress, the long list of possible gene influencers includes diet, smoking, and other unhealthy lifestyle factors. Imagine, then, minute to minute, what our minds could be up against while potentially under the influence of all that extra 'baggage?'

If our parents, grandparents or great-grandparents survived slavery, poverty, famine, war, persecution, rape, spousal abuse, the death of a child, genocide, abandonment, or any horrific event before they bore their children, what did they pass down to us? What are we all dealing with? It is almost certain that every day, we are working with and against unknown, unexplainable, and undiagnosable imbalances. The good news is we can maintain hope for the future. Experts report that a positive mental state can *also* influence our genes, helping to restore the balance between our bodies and psyches. And this makes sense because *if our bodies can become altered through negative means, we should absolutely be able to alter them through positive!*

To consistently stay in a chosen state of mind and being by purposefully re-directing our internal and external dialogue—this is an important aspect of PM. One way we can do this is to constantly read, listen to, and speak positive and reinforcing words, messages, phrases, prayers, mantras, sounds, tones, and songs. This deliberate action can help every cell in our bodies resonate with the state of being we choose to be in rather than the state we have acquired. The more consistently we use PM, the more opportunity we have to influence and improve the state of our psyches and genetic predispositions. It is like being on a journey back to authenticity... back to being the loving and healthy beings we were created to be. And we can label this practice Positive Manipulation®, or we can call it sound healing, tuning, mindfulness, meditation, surrendering, or devotional prayer. We can rely on the Holiness of our God, other Divine Being, the Angels, Saints, Universe, or our Souls—no matter how we worship or choose to stay spiritually centered, it will all work as long as our motive is pure. *When we act from love and goodness, we will see Love and Goodness in action,* and isn't that what every faith and religion have in common: the need to stay connected to the principles of love and goodness? Isn't love what all humans are consistently striving for?

Gregg Braden, best-selling author and pioneer in bridging science and spirituality, speaks publicly about love's potential: *"When we choose to feel feelings such as love, appreciation, gratitude, forgiveness, care, and compassion, they create coherence (unity of our physical, mental, emotional, and spiritual selves), and when we can feel those feelings, they are mirrored in 'The Field' and everyone benefits from the experience of the relatively few."* He contends that we can create this effect with the square root of one percent of any given population. Let's consider for a moment what this expert is saying… When you and I generate love and peace within ourselves, we will each have a positive effect on 100 people in our energetic sphere of influence. When 100 of us come together for the same purpose, we can influence 10,000 others. Envision, then, the possibilities of 7,000 citizens— purportedly the square root of one percent of our world's population—doing this… To borrow John Lennon's words, *"Imagine all the people…!"*

To quickly summarize what Braden called "The Field," in 1944, Max Planck, said to be the father of quantum theory, called this network of energy we all share "The Matrix." Others call it "The

Mind of Nature," and depending on who I am speaking with, I refer to it as *Our System* or *God's System* because using the word system implies that something came into existence for our use and benefit, freedom of will, and most especially, potential. It would seem, fellow journeyer, that this universe and its vast complexities are here for us to work *with,* not just for us to dwell *in.*

> *"The future depends on what we do in the present."*
> **Mahatma Gandhi**

Does *'matter'* really matter?

As stated before, science now accepts that all things (seen or unseen) are energy, not matter. Again, this is nothing new; the Bible may be referencing 'energy' in many of its scriptures (Genesis 3:19, Colossians 1:29, and Galatians 5:22 are just a few), and scholars such as Socrates pitched the energy concept thousands of years ago. It is important for you and me to embrace this finding now because through our understanding we can finally start using our spiritual gifts properly!

Since it has been reported that we are made of sound, light, and what is called scalar energy, it is appropriate to believe we are always sitting in, emanating out, and reacting to frequencies of energy. According to quantum experts, each of our bodies' cells, every organ, and all our thoughts and emotions (what we call feelings) are generating their own, individual electromagnetic frequencies (EMFs). All EMFs influence each another and then co-mingle with the energy field being influenced and energized by what is emanating from everything in the universe and on Earth.

To make things even more complicated, we have unseen influencers at work that stem from the deeper part of our psyche called "the subconscious mind." Freud, the founder of psychoanalysis, compared our conscious and subconscious states to an iceberg, stating that consciousness—the ten percent tip of the iceberg—houses the thoughts and feelings we are aware of, as well as our memories and stored knowledge. He claimed the other ninety percent hidden below the surface is where we house the potential for *deep fears, shame, unacceptable sexual impulses, violent motives, irrational wishes, selfish needs, and immoral urges.* It is presumed that everything buried there is the cumulative result of events that occurred in the womb all the way through adulthood. (And now that we know about epigenetic inheritance, perhaps our parents, grandparents, and ancestors' experiences could be housed there as well?)

The scariest aspect of the subconscious is that it is as its name implies; "sub". The only way we can tell if we have anything harmful and damaging *down there* is by consciously witnessing drama and trauma playing out *up here* in our daily lives. We should assume that if we are consistently trying to manipulate out of certain bad habits, mindsets, old belief systems, and feelings without success; if we are doing everything we can to be successful and we are still not living the life we want or attracting the opportunities and relationships we desire, we will have to heal from past traumas, inherited 'stuff,' and whatever else exists in that ninety-percent hidden in the subconscious mind. We would also have to address the potential for the people, animals, and things we come in contact with, as well as the environment, the chemistry in what we consume, our own biochemistry and hormones, and even the moon and other planets to occasionally whack out our bodies and wig out our moods, making healing and restoration even more difficult.

Energy that exists will persist until we change it, but this is when Positive Manipulation® can help us. When we create a willful intention to be our best selves, we will feel instinctively led to understanding and healing even that which we cannot see or initially comprehend. It is then that intuition—*the part of us that is timeless and connected to all that is greater than we are* —will take the lead. It all comes down to this: *No 'matter' we are dealing with in our physical lives can create a problem for us that energy can't fix!*

The *Gooder* the Better!

Throughout my Christian upbringing, I was told to "love thy neighbor, be good, and act as an 'extension' of God." Leave it to my dyslexic brain to literally picture Go_d. So, essentially, when I *was* being an extension, I thought I was putting the extra "o" in the word Go<u>o</u>d! A silly visual, for sure, but it served me well over the years as a human and a coach. I have found that, irrespective of my clients' spiritual, religious, or non-religious backgrounds, if I suggest they create a daily intention to be and do their best and they willingly accept the challenge, they start moving quickly down the road to wellness, steering themselves toward exponential growth and spiritual advancement. It would seem that *Goodness is universal and has its own energetic prowess!* And why not; it is, after all, something every human wants returning to them. But the real benefit for those of us who take this daily journey is a deeper sense and knowingness that we become 'greater' as we attach ourselves to the greater source of love and goodness already in existence.

Something else I have noticed: even when we aren't strong enough to stay loving and good all the time, we are gently steered back and very quickly, too, in an unconditionally loving way. The voice I hear in my right ear never utters a single word of judgment for the crazy circumstances I sometimes create for myself. (Although I have caught some chortling on occasion and an "Oh, Donna, really?" more than a few times!)

After years of using and teaching the *SuperCharging* powers of PM, I can honestly say the results are remarkable. Stories of triumph over issues in relationships, career, and money are routinely reported, as well as the release of sorrow, *un*forgiveness, anger, and harmful and counter-productive emotions, habits, and addictions. Each person professes to feel more love and a newfound awareness and appreciation of all there is out there for us to tap into. Our System that we can all benefit from—it's so simple to use even though it's so complicated to figure out! Lucky for us, we don't need to understand all of it in order to reap the loving rewards it offers.

"And I say to you, I have also decided to stick to love. For I know that love is ultimately the only answer to mankind's problems. And I'm going to talk about it everywhere I go. I know it isn't popular to talk about it in some circles today. I'm not talking about emotional bosh when I talk about love, I'm talking about a strong, demanding love ... I am convinced that love is the most durable power in the world. It is not an expression of impractical idealism, but of practical realism. Far from being the pious injunction of a Utopian dreamer, love is an absolute necessity for the survival of our civilization." **Dr. Martin Luther King, Jr.**

"Earth to Soul, come in Soul!"

To stay connected to love and goodness (the higher aspects of ourselves), we have to make a conscious effort to do so minute to minute; sometimes, second to second. That is PM, and there are only two pre-requisites needed to start: (1) We must *take responsibility* for everything we are and everything we do *without laying fault or blame* on ourselves or others, and (2) We must *step into our lives on purpose each day intending and willing to be and do our best.* That's it! That is all we seem to need to stay connected to our Souls, goals, and Higher Knowing.

Please notice I wrote, "*without laying fault or blame…*" Consider all of the influences every one of us has been dealing with since inception and beyond —the 'baggage' we may be toting around each day as described on pages 18 and 19. When we come together with that baggage, as it is commonly expressed, "Sh#% happens!" We need to be mindful that each of us is dealing with circumstances and situations the only way our physical, emotional, mental, and spiritual wherewithal will allow. Sometimes that makes us seem like an offender; sometimes like a victim, but we can't stay as either and then seek victory. We need to make the decision to take responsibility for our participation in all our life episodes because as soon as we do, our perception and emotions become under our control. And in that moment of control, we connect with the part of ourselves more attuned to our best outcome.

Making room in our hearts for love and forgiveness and keeping our minds attuned to personal responsibility—both seem a small price to pay for a *SuperCharged* life! But more importantly, both are essential mindsets that lead to rectifying any 'energetic pull' that keeps us too grounded in humanness and too far from Soul.

Choosing to Dumb it Down

Human knowledge is limited so remaining open-minded and humble is important. I jokingly refer to myself as being dumb as a stump because *I'm smart enough to know that I'm not smart enough to know everything!* Even ten PhDs can't help someone know it all, but when we willfully decide to let go of how we, in our simply human state, think things should progress, we immediately allow for our Higher Knowing and Power to inspire us. The reality is that no matter what we lack in understanding, IQ, or education, we can grow wiser and advance in miraculous ways. When in doubt of this, try to rely upon an important aspect of your human potential: *You don't have to know how to get to your best life; you just have to want it and will it every day, and the steps you need to take will become obvious as you move and grow forward, spiritually lifting all along the way.*

Whether we are led to an expert in trauma therapy, a new diet, drug, or vitamin that balances hormones and biochemistry, a doctor who will diagnose a mysterious disorder, a healer who teaches self-help techniques, a therapy geared toward overcoming betrayal, an addiction counselor, spiritual coach, priest, pastor, rabbi, church, mosque, synagogue, temple, religious center, meditation retreat, article, scripture, video, movie, song, or a book just like this one... All the ways and means to move forward will be afforded to us when we take responsibility and humbly ask ourselves to see and hear what is needed to advance.

As I stated on page 27, the second step in initiating the process of PM is to create an intention each day to be the best we can be. We do this because we can strive for something better, but we may not know how far we can actually go. Labeling it as "the best" will bring us to a level of advancement that is achievable that day without putting limitations on what else is possible. That intention, by the way, reinforces our goals, and goal setting has two aspects to consider: (1) *what we want to achieve* and (2) *the reason why we want to achieve it*. As a reminder, while I was going through my divorce, I desired to be more loving and forgiving and to be the best mom I could possibly be. I also created financial and wellness goals so I could take care of my family as a single parent.

After setting them, I expressly stated my motive was for the sake of my kids. My esteem was so low I didn't even desire a better life for myself, but I knew I had to make things better for them. My heartfelt need to be the best I could be and to achieve symbiotic outcomes—I believe this is what initiated the download of wisdom and direction I received.

The self-manipulation process (getting over my human/ego self) brought empowerment to every minute of each day making me realize that when our minds' thoughts, hearts' emotions, and Souls' intuition are engaged and working on our goals together, we can't help but succeed at everything we do. Even when we occasionally react to our human wants and cravings, the goodness and power behind the goal and motive will eventually win out. Every situation we face will break down to a choice—a PM moment of who we should listen to, our very human/ego self or our spiritually empowered Soul. That decision acts as a switch and when flipped to Soul, instantly changes our state of being, each situation's outcome, and the direction we are headed.

It is important to note here that *when we positively manipulate our own energy, we aren't manipulating others.* Rightfully, **we can't manipulate anyone else and call it positive.** *We can only instigate positive change in our own minds, hearts, and bodies. That action changes the energy we share with others and* *will initiate the potential for a better response from them.* It is always up to the other person how they intend to act and react, and whether they are willing to accept what we are soulfully and lovingly offering. In all my years practicing and teaching this technique, though, I have never known a loving intention to *not* instigate a more positive result. If doing so didn't seem to immediately help the other person or the relationship, it definitely achieved a spontaneous and favorable effect on the person who initiated the act of love.

When Faking is Good Practice

Dr. Wayne Dyer: *"You'll see it when you believe it!"* Buddha: *"The mind is everything. What you think you become!"* And God, as written in Mark 11:24: *"Therefore I tell you, whatever you ask in prayer, believe that you have received it, and it will be yours."* … So many teachings that remind us to have faith in what we can achieve, yet we still doubt ourselves and the powers that be! Even the scientific claims about the positive physical effects of mindfulness, prayer, meditation, and sound healing haven't convinced the majority of the world's population that our minds and voices can influence our bodies, emotions, and every other aspect of our lives. Isn't it time we finally admit to ourselves that every day we don't utilize our spiritual gifts, we are wasting *good* potential?

People ask me all the time, "What if I want to give this process an earnest try but still doubt it can help me; should I say the mantras anyway, faking it until the rest of me catches up?" My answer is yes! Remember what I previously wrote about the cells in our bodies… that they are responding to what we tell them? Well, 'faking it' is just a form of PM that can override the ego-driven mentality that leads us to believe we can't do what we really *can* do. Some may disagree with this type of mind manipulation, but my experience has shown it to be quite empowering.

As a child and all the way through my senior year in high school, I dealt with undiagnosed dyslexia. From tying my own shoes and learning the alphabet, to riding a bike and playing sports, I was often teased and labeled "the dumb one" because I struggled immensely through every new learning experience. There were times I was reprimanded by teachers and (let's remember this was in the 1960s and 70s) even slapped for my lack of concentration or comprehension. Out of fear, I often resorted to fibbing—telling my teachers I could do something, even though I wasn't sure how, or saying I understood, even when I didn't. Afterward, I would retreat to a safe place to figure it all out.

My little body was in a constant state of fear, anxiety, self-doubt, and confusion that presented as "yucky bubbles in my belly." I couldn't let those bubbles stop me, though, as failure was never an option. In order to survive, I changed the I-can't-do-this thoughts in my head to "I think I can, I think I can, I think I can…" Borrowed from my favorite storybook "The Little Engine That Could," this audible and visual reminder kept me steadfast because I believed if she could climb the mountain, so could I. That, and my willingness to be good, always seemed to lead to an appropriate outcome.

Back then, I had no idea I was using a mantra to 'fake myself out' of my emotions. In fact, until my forties, I didn't even realize it had become a way of life. The offshoot was that I grew quite fearless. From building a house when we needed a place to live, to starting my own business after being wrongfully fired, I just envisioned the destination and refused to let fear (of how I was going to get there) stop me. From past experience, "I knew I could, I knew I could, I knew I could" eventually find my way clear. It would seem that my *childhood dyslexia— which made everything into a challenge I was forced to overcome—left me as an adult with the belief that nothing was really a challenge anymore.* It was just a goal that dared me to discover new ways to maneuver my brain and overcome my fears. Truthfully, I'm more afraid now of saying no to my goals and the promptings of my Soul. I truly believe *it is our earnest effort that equates to success. Our only failure would be to never try.*

And then came my biggest and most frightening challenge; namely, Crohn's Disease, and in 2009, mantras and my fake-it-till-I-make-it way of thinking actually saved my life. Allow me to use illness as an example of how initially fibbing to ourselves can move us toward our desired outcome: Let's say we are sick and want to heal but when speaking the phrase "I am healthy," we feel disingenuous, unworthy, or consider ourselves to be lying or in denial of the illness. What I am suggesting (and what I believe Mark 11:24 implies) is to *step into our future declaring the state of being we desire to be in.* With conviction, we say, "I am healed; I am well," because we *are* intending to heal, right? We are *willing* to become healthy, aren't we? To overcome any doubt that our cells will eventually listen to our minds, we should add this precursory statement: "My body is always restoring itself!" We say this because it is scientific, and it is real.

The truth is we *are* magnificent, self-healing machines! Our bodies' cells are constantly trying to regenerate and repair. We come equipped with this built-in ability, and people from all over the world have healed, been successfully compensating for, and even been cured of almost every physical, emotional, and mental condition in existence. I relied heavily on this information when doctors gave me a scary

34

prognosis based on what other patients in my situation had experienced. I believed I could do it though; I could maintain my body's health if I kept envisioning myself teaching yoga and Pilates, hiking, writing, public speaking—living the thriving, unencumbered lifestyle I knew I was meant to live. I was convinced that *the doctors knew the disease and how to medically treat it, but it was my responsibility to heal from it!* When I announced my plan of treatment, they felt obligated to tell me that the odds were 90% against me. I won't lie; that percentage shook my resolve, but as fate would dictate, my young, talented surgeon, Dr. Anna, saw the odds differently. "I've known you for months now," she said, "I've seen what you've come through, and nothing keeps you down…" Her encouraging words captured my attention, but what she said next was spoken with such soulful conviction, an indelible impression was left—one I will reference for years to come: "Donna," she declared, "even if only a one percent chance of success existed, *YOU* would be that one percent! You can do this!"

The best part about that day—she was right. Ultimately, no advice or diagnosis was ignored, nor was the disease hated or 'fought.' I have learned to bring love and understanding to the parts of my body that need my help, and taking responsibility for my health has led to a greater understanding of how this autoimmune disease is triggered and why it originally developed. Today, I still manipulate any doubts in my mind by repeating mantras and imagining my desired outcome, which guides me toward the best treatments, foods, and lifestyle choices. Through meditation and prayer, I ask what can I do to stay balanced; then I listen, stepping into each new day on purpose, willing to do what I am being shown. Bottom line, *I choose to have faith in the powers that be; I choose to believe in me!* And I should let you know that before I had this conviction or the help of Dr. Anna, I was suffering greatly, barely subsisting and with no human will left in me, but something beyond my understanding still guided my journey.

I'll never forget the early spring day I laid in bed in horrific pain just staring at the dormant maple tree outside my window. After enduring months of my own lifelessness, I announced to God, "You can take me now; I'm ready." I vowed not to stick around to see that tree bloom. For some reason, though, I couldn't help visualizing it with green buds; then the buds became leaves, and before long, my mind brought it back to life. It was then that something ethereal became visible in the corner of my bedroom. It spoke to me and was there to let me know "this is not your time to go." I asked why and was reminded of my purpose and then given a writing assignment —my reason to keep living. I felt energized by the news, and so I dialed the phone laying next to me. Barely able to whisper, I asked my son to take me to the hospital, and upon arrival, doctors and nurses brought me back to life. It would seem that I had less than half the blood and iron I needed to survive.

Disease, it can be said, is the perfect storm, and practitioners, scientists, and researchers from esteemed hospitals and research facilities all over the world know and understand that all aspects of ourselves—the physical, mental, emotional, and spiritual—are constantly influencing one another. These experts agree that a patient's state of mind is crucial, and many will back me up on this—what I have consistently found to be true: *If we tell ourselves with belief that we are healthy, our bodies start to respond by healing themselves; tell ourselves with belief that we are sick, and our bodies will act accordingly.* When sickness takes hold, we must stand convicted in the belief that we (and add your divine being/co-creating partner here) are stronger than whatever our body is experiencing. What I say about Crohn's now: *"I may have had it, but it never had me!"* Disease has occasionally taken up space in my body, but I don't allow it to take up space in my mind. The fact is our bodies, goals, relationships—every part of our physical and spiritual lives—need our help. No matter what our faith predicates, we must be willing to keep our thoughts and emotions focused on our desired outcome. No matter where we find ourselves physically planted at this moment—whether it is a cozy couch or a hospital bed, a beautiful home or a jail cell, at work or standing in line at the unemployment office—we have to mentally convince ourselves right now that our minds and hearts are powerful tools wrapped in remarkably comprehensive packages. When you are in doubt of this, remember: *No one—not one scientist, doctor or human—knows what you are capable of, not even you!* When it comes down to it, miracles do happen. How to bring about a miracle is what has always been in question... perhaps until now.

They may be mini, but they are still Mighty!

It will be your dedication to being the best "you" you are willing to be that will ultimately prompt your lift, but these mantras can assist you. They were designed to help you maintain a positive state of being, trigger your own innate wisdom, instigate your body's own natural healing potential, and keep you blissfully connected to your spiritual self. To keep things simple, I made them simple, but they are still very powerful, positive suggestions that will help you override whatever perceived negativity you may be experiencing. If you still find yourself questioning whether short sentences about love, goodness, and personal responsibility have the potential to help you re-direct your disposition or change your habits, cells, genes, or subconscious mind, please understand: The underlying edifice of each musing (the message and mantra combined) was built on fifty-eight years of experience, study, spiritual download, and soul-searching. And when I had my own doubts or trouble understanding a concept, I researched it ad nauseam for the purpose of sharing with you what is believed to be real and true.

Know that our hearts and brains were designed to emanate thoughts and emotions that are said to be as *mighty* as almost any force found in the universe. And as quantum expert Dr. Joe Dispenza puts it, *"No human is so special that he or she does not possess this capability!"* So, fellow journeyer, take comfort in the knowledge that the concepts in this book—coupled with your own self-help techniques, innate wisdom, and faith—can keep your head and heart generating the most profound and positive energy you can possibly share with this world!

"Until you transcend the ego, you can do nothing but add to the insanity of the world." **Dr. Wayne Dyer**

Staying the Course

Even with all this potential at our disposal, it is possible that the process of change might, at times, seem too difficult, challenging, or scary. If this rings true for you, consider what your life would be like if you remained right where you are and as you are... Is this in your best interest? Staying stuck in a painful past and denying our symptoms, true nature, destiny, or Soul's promptings... all of this can cause mental, emotional, and physical stress. It can feel extremely uncomfortable and exhausting, possibly causing depression or, as in my case, even lead to disease. It can feel like pushing the weight of an enormous boulder that is bearing down on our body and Soul. I call this energy-draining state of unwillingness, *ego resistance*, and it seems to force us into some sort of *spiritual repression*, making it almost impossible for us to connect to our Higher Knowing and Power.

So you understand, I don't believe our power sources ever detach from us, but we humans certainly have the ability to detach from our sources of power! Addressing denial seems to be the only way to come out of ego resistance and spiritual repression. If we want to hear what is trying to come into our right ear, we have to change the unproductive mindsets and emotions that are holding us in abeyance. After years of dealing with denial in myself and those I've coached, I've come to learn it just isn't worth ignoring or negating the loving, truth-seeking, forgiving, altruistic voice and what it prompts us to do. We need to consistently remind ourselves that *denial is a terrible thing to waste* because what we are in denial of could actually be what we need to see in order to reach our goals and live happily and productively.

Another reason we hold ourselves back is lack of self-love and self-worth. If this is the case for you, think about starting the same as I did by doing it for your loved ones, or do it for your God and the world because we all deserve to know and see the best of who you really are. Your self-evaluation will evolve as you lovingly let go of the ego voice that devalues and limits your worth and potential. Choose to give your human self a rest while you allow the mastery of your Higher Knowing and Power to guide each minute of all your days ahead.

When you set your intention to step into today making the best decisions and desiring to live your best life in the best body you can achieve, then you need to know that you are already *there;* already accomplishing it because every minute from this moment forward, you are becoming better and better at being *You.* No more negative outlook or come-what-may attitude about how your day will unfold, either, because you already know where you are heading. The truth is *you can't help but walk into the future you are mentally and emotionally preparing for.*

PART II

How to Use This Book

Mighty Mindsets

When I named this book, "My Mini..." it was meant for you to make it *yours*. As I have stated, though, your openness to using it... *that* is what will ultimately determine how effective the mantras and the Positive Manipulation® process are for you. Hopefully, you will make the decision to incorporate both into your daily routine, but if you find yourself initially challenging, disagreeing with, or not believing some of what you are reading, take pause. You *should* question what feels uncomfortable; you should question me! But before you allow doubt to take hold, question yourself. Discomfort might occur for two reasons: (1) Intuition... what you are reading doesn't resonate as the truth or goes against your religious beliefs, and (2) An emotional trigger...what you are feeling is preventing you from taking your next step. Mentally ask yourself which fits, and remain open to hearing the answer. If you sense it is the first reason, please remember, everything written here was meant for you to customize to your own religious beliefs and teachings. There is no arrogance intended—spiritual or otherwise. Even the word mantra can be exchanged for the word prayer, and every sentence can include your Divine Being. Still, you may want to seek religious or spiritual guidance, pray, meditate, research, or write me for further clarification of my intention to literally put us all on the same page about love and goodness.

Now, if your discomfort stems from the second reason, ask for the strength to see and work through your trigger, then go back to the mantra after seeking expert advice or when you feel led to. (Remember, just being willing to face a challenge prepares us to be ready and able to take it on.) During this manipulation process, it is imperative to be firm with yourself but not harsh or self-deprecating. Louise Hay, the famous author and spiritualist, told us to *"be kind to our mind."* She said, *"We need to build instead of beat down."* When you look back on your past, make a conscious effort to take the best of what it has to offer. *If what went on back then was important enough to experience, it is important enough now to learn and heal from.* You need to love yourself without guilt through the process of growth and self-healing so every circumstance going forward will be as productive, loving, and positive as it can be.

Using Our Voice as a Healing Tool

It is important to understand why I use the word 'Mantra'. It means tool or instrument of the mind. So, suffice it to say, it perfectly compliments the rebuilding process we are undertaking. Mantras include a syllable, word, phrase, prayer, or statement that is repeated over and over through thought, voice, music, and sound, You will notice in Part III that every paragraph is a stand-alone, which I have referred to as *a musing*. Each musing contains two parts: the message and that is typed in regular font, followed by the mantra, which can be combined with prayer. These are in quotes and typed in ***bold italic***. (Please note that a few mantras stand alone.) Feel free to utilize your favorite method of conveyance; meaning, speak it, chant it, sing it, hum it while you think it, play an instrument as you vocalize, or put on ambient music in the background. Sometimes, I blow on my harmonica as I meditate on the words. It doesn't matter that I don't really know how to play it! Music is said to be the heart's native language, so I allow my instincts to guide the notes I play. If you do not own or have access to an instrument, use a pot as a drum, or search for sources of healing music and sound frequencies online.

Some people record themselves repeating their chosen mantra so when speaking out loud is not an option, they can use earplugs and meditate to the sound of their own voice. Our ancestors—ancient Egyptians, Greeks, and other indigenous tribes from around the globe—used their voices in healing ceremonies. Called vocal toning, it was recently proven to have a positive impact on different body systems. In fact, by just vocalizing the eight vowel sounds or musical notes from mid C to G, we can influence our heart rate, blood pressure, lymphatic system, levels of serotonin and melatonin, as well as our release of oxytocin. And why wouldn't this body manipulation technique work; we are, after all, made of sound energy!

Another way to execute mantras is to repeat them while we work, walk, hike, dance, exercise, or partake in any physical activity. Amazingly enough, the part of our brain that controls planned movement is the same part of our brain that controls thinking. Evidence shows that moving while we are trying to learn or memorize information will substantially increase our ability to understand and retain it. Imagine the possibilities, especially for our children, if we combined physical movement with every study experience… Visualize an entire classroom of third graders balancing in tree pose while reciting the multiplication table… How much more prolific, fun, and exciting would and could learning be?

Engage in any and all of these methods to help make your mantras go from words you are reading to beliefs your entire being can accept. As you repeat them daily, notice the calming effect they have on your mind and body; it will be tangible and according to the Department of Neurobiology at the Weizmann Institute of Science in Israel, this effect can be seen on an MRI of the brain. Essentially, repeating positive words helps to convert the negative noise in our heads that makes us physically and emotionally uncomfortable. (Revisit page 21 for more information on "coherence.")

After some time and practice, what is repeated will also leave an impression on our subconscious. Just like everything else that ends up there, the positive phrases will eventually become subliminal. You may actually hear them as if they were playing on a tape recorder in the back of your mind. The hope is that as you are going about your day (and most specifically when you are being challenged and in dire need of a soulful boost) you will hear exactly what you need to create your new perception, thoughts, and moods.

Understanding What You are Reading

There are three categories for the musings you will find in this book: *realizations, reminders,* and *remedies. Realizations* can be ah-ha moments or wake-up calls that help us understand our potential and how powerful our minds and hearts truly are. *Reminders* will mentally and emotionally bring us back to awareness (what we already know or believe to be true). And *remedies* offer us ways to manipulate, renegotiate, redirect, or replace ineffective physical, mental, and emotional energy (what is not working for our higher good). How we perceive each musing will depend on our state of awareness. And many musings will seem similar to one another; that is deliberate. Certain mindsets are pivotal to sustainable growth and through experience, I've discovered that we humans learn best when information is inculcated. In other words, repetition is sometimes necessary, so try to think of each day's mantra as a pearl on a string. Once they are strung together, you will have a more complete creation.

And taking into consideration that this is *your* creation, please note that there are empty spaces left purposefully on the bottom of some pages so you can write your own inspired musings and prayers. As a reminder: whatever you write and repeat should be positive, loving, and rooted in goodness, because every*thing* and every *person* existing in your inner and outer worlds are responding energetically to your thoughts, emotions, and beliefs. It is crucial that you concentrate on what it is that you *want* to see, not on what you don't want to see; what you love, not what you hate; what you want to reap, not what you don't want to be sowed. Be the architect of your future by creating the mental imagery of the life you are building for yourself. Realize that wanting will keep you wanting, so believe instead that you already have or are already in the state of being you visualize yourself to be in. If you find yourself consistently using the words want, wish, or need, make sure you follow them with "I am...!" Then back these statements up with some gratitude for what is here and what is forthcoming. (For more information on "I am," refer to pages 115 and 163.)

Daily Instruction

My suggestion before making your selection is to create an uplifting, loving intention to hear and see what you need to successfully step into that new day. Then pick a page number, thumb, or scroll through the pages if it's an ebook, allowing yourself to be guided by goodness, God, or the Higher Power of *your* understanding. When you come upon a musing that feels right (resonates internally), make it your day's recitation. Remember, if reading that musing makes you uncomfortable, ask why and wait for an answer. If the mantra's message is something you don't believe in or aren't ready to accept, bypass it and choose another. If you don't like the way the mantra is worded, rewrite it to suit your personality. This can't be stressed enough: It is your book and your journey! Spend some time personalizing your mantras by writing in God, Krishna, Allah, Universe, Light, or the specific Divine Being and deity you worship, pray to, co-create and align with. Each musing has been carefully written to be appropriate for all belief systems that are rooted in love and goodness. As long as the reciter stays centered in love, the mantras should be considered complementary to their faith.

You may want to tag, bookmark, or highlight your new day's musing in some way. There are also blank index pages in the back of your book so you can keep track of page numbers and favorites for quick reference. When there is a need to really drive a message home, repeating the mantra for three days will help the brain and heart create a new connection. Rewrite the mantra or type it into your phone so you can refer to it often. To bring more power to this process, speak the entire mantra— mentally and out loud—as often as you can during waking hours and right before bed. When appropriate, I act out the words by getting up and making grand gestures with my hands and arms when I speak the statement, "*I am love personified!*" I stand in Superman pose (scientifically proven to boost confidence) when I declare I am "*flowing with power!*" And I physically move forward when I announce, "*I step into my life on purpose!*" Since light energy exists within us, I take advantage by imagining radiant beams of red light 'pouring' from my heart when I want to send unconditional love and forgiveness to someone. I'll picture white, violet, or gold penetrating my head from Source while green healing light flows up from the Earth into my body. Throughout the Bible, colors have been known to be symbolic of different virtues, and psychology experts have reported the effect each hue has on our moods. Science has also uncovered different properties, strengths, and benefits of each, so doing a little research, if you are so inclined, is worth the effort.

Combining mantras with physical and visual action fortifies your intentions and puts your entire being into the process. It also offers more potential to override any doubt—real or subconscious—that you have the ability to rehabilitate, restore, and rejuvenate yourself. Remember, with certainty, this detail of your humanity: *Your body will believe what you tell it; your mind will follow your Soul if you let it!*

It is important to note that some mantras may take longer to sink in than others. Consider reciting them for an entire week or more if you feel led to or until you feel a shift occurring in your psyche. (And when that happens, you will know!) During this extension of time, you may still wake up in the morning and want or feel led to select an additional mantra. Past experience has shown me that they build on one another. As long as the person using them is well-intentioned and connected to their intuitive self, there should be no worry of overloading on the energy that repeating and layering the mantras will produce.

Expecting Change

Consistent with any change in energy, life, as usual, may change. Growing pains are real and can actually prevent some people from continuing on their wellness journey. If you start to experience discomfort, realize that as you become more authentic, so too will your circumstances. As you grow, it stands to reason that some of your relationships will evolve as well. Your spiritual gifts and intuition will expand, making you more sensitive to the truth and untruths you encounter during your day-to-day experiences. Anyone and anything not in alignment with the beautiful life you are trying to create will be brought to light. Some habits, people, places, and things may need to go or will leave on their own. Discomfort about these changes is normal, but try to view what is transpiring as a result of the powerful, positive forward movement you are creating. And perhaps you will want some things to stay the same! Know that they can because you are in control of stopping and starting this process.

Acknowledge, though, when *you* are holding *you* back, and if someone or something else is standing in the way of your advancement, deal with such as you become ready, willing, and able. Again, it is always your choice how far and how fast you travel. And most importantly, remember that *the road to wellness is not paved by perfection*; in fact, it is not paved at all. It unfurls itself day by day as each journeyer chooses to walk upon it. It is not intended to make its travelers into model humans, either! Its purpose is to promote optimal health, happiness, and balance, which can only be achieved when our minds, bodies, and Souls are in alignment and in the moment. Know that *You* create this walkway for yourself, every day, each step, all along the way. It can look like anything you want it to look like and take you anywhere *you* want to go.

A final word of support: try carrying your mini book with you as a physical reminder of your power, purpose, and potential. Optimistically, it will help you stay focused on your intent as you *grow forward* in the best direction your inner guidance system wants to take you. ♥

Now, let's begin…

PART III

MESSAGES AND MANTRAS

*"Being born was our gift.
Living life is our challenge.
Being the best we can be is our choice."*
Donna Martini

Whatever we do and say is a reflection of who we really are. We need to decide each day what thoughts and emotions we show the world. *"Mindful and 'heartful' of how I present myself."*

Since it is impossible for both love and *un*forgiveness to occupy the same space, we need to let go of one to make room for the other. To tap into our most potent and positive energy, we must clear out the not-so-positive emotions we are holding onto. *"My heart expands with love."*

Too much body without spirit and we cannot lift. Too much spirit without body and we cannot ground. Tranquility, peace, and our greatest potential lies in the space between our humanness and soulfulness. We can gain access to that space by taking deep breaths while requesting of ourselves to *"Align body... align mind... align Soul."*

If we want to show and tell the world how powerful we really are, we need to approach life with our most positive and powerful attitude. Then, we have to walk that internal talk, or no one will listen. *"I am a walking/talking billboard of my beliefs and passions."*

Self-love is a gift our Souls give to our human selves every day but all too often, we find it hard to accept. Today, we can change that! *"I'm accepting the love being offered."*

The way the world views us is based on how we view the world. If we want to leave our most favorable impression, we can make the effort to *"See the good in everyone and everything today."*

If we are feeling afraid, we will create the energy of fear, and we will draw to ourselves that which we fear! Instead of constantly walking into what we *don't* want, we need to concentrate on and believe in our ability to—each and every day—walk into what we *do* want. *"Faithful and fearless."*

The universe is reflecting back to us everything we are sending out. We need to consistently create and recite the thoughts and emotions we want to be returned to us. *"Generating positive, beautiful sentiments."*

To thine own self be true; but, unless we ask, how can we be sure what our true self really wants? Today, we can put all ego wants, needs, fears, anger, and triggers aside so we can hear and see all that our true self wants to reveal. *"I am listening."*

We look with our eyes, hear with our ears, and speak with our mouths, but if we do all three without enlisting our hearts, nothing will be worth seeing, hearing or speaking. *"My **heart** is engaged!"*

If a feeling is a thought combined with emotion, then we should decide to let our hearts tell our minds that we are *"Feeling happy today!"*

No need to fret, regret, or forget the past. If what went on back then was important enough to experience, it is important enough now to learn and heal from. Decide: *"I'm growing forward and taking the best of my past with me."*

Let's choose to step into the world equipped with a sword of truth and a shield of love. With truth and love, we are always protected!

"Armed and ready for anything!"

$\mathcal{N}$ote to My Ego Self: *"Please stay out of my way today. I've got a lot of accomplishing to do!"*

$\mathcal{O}$ur heads judge; our hearts emote; our guts will react. Our reality is based on one, two, or all three of these perceptions, but is this 'reality' based on truth? We need to purposefully ask our very human selves to put opinions, emotions, and reactions aside in favor of hearing, seeing, and feeling our Souls' viewpoint. That decision will bring us to a new reality filled with tolerance, compassion, and love. Whether to act very human or incredibly soulful… it's always our choice what side of ourselves we engage. *"Driving on Soul-fuel today."*

$\mathcal{W}$e should accept responsibility for everything that happens in our lives because when we take responsibility, we take control, and as soon as we take control, we have the power and ability to create positive change. To achieve the best outcome for every circumstance, self-reflect and ask, *"What did I contribute to this scenario?"*

Our old, negative belief systems are like cesspools; they hold what we no longer need. Every minute of every day we can choose to release all that is clogging the flow in our hearts, minds, and lives. *"I willingly release what I no longer need!"*

Lies we tell and lies we hear create energy that travels through and effects every cell in our body, making us weak and uncomfortable. Truth affects our cells too, but it creates an energy that leads to strength, assuredness, and security. *"Choosing to be immersed in and surrounded by the truth."*

We honor our bodies by giving them the nutrition and exercise they need. We honor our minds by filling them with positive thoughts. We honor our souls by listening to them. *"I'm 'hear' for you."*

Accepting responsibility for what went on in our past should not make us feel or think we are laying fault or blame on ourselves. Instead, we should view it as a crucial step toward mental empowerment, spiritual awareness, and emotional freedom. *"Willingly accepting the role I played; steering my way into to a beautiful new future."*

We are one with the Earth and made of the same molecules, nutrients, and minerals. There is no separation between us unless we create it. When we put our bare feet in the Earth's bounty, we energetically connect to a power far greater than ourselves. Earth's negative charge will right our physical wrongs as its essence fills us with peace and joy. Today, find a beach, a forest, or some dirt, grass, or rocks to connect with; barefooted, stand firmly and repeat: *"Plugging into power!"*

We 'know' more as spiritual beings through intuition than we could ever think with our human intellect, so *"Stop thinking and start knowing."*

We can wait and hope for our lives to change on their own, or we can be willing to be the change our lives have been waiting for... *"Be the hope; be the change."*

When we decide to take judgment and ridicule out of our heads, we allow the truth about everything we are experiencing to come right in. *"Truth be known!"*

$\mathcal{N}$ote to My Ego Self: Since when did we become their judge and jury? Let's have respect and stop rubber-necking on another person's journey. *"Look ahead and move forward on our own."*

$\mathcal{P}$ositive Manipulation® is a mental and spiritual process we can undertake which, with one decision, can instantly convert any unhealthy and unproductive physical, emotional, and mental state we find ourselves in, into something healthy and worthwhile. We start the process daily by choosing to be the best we can be. We keep it going every day the same exact way. *"Willfully choosing to be my best self."*

$\mathcal{W}$hen we find ourselves spinning in the same cycle of drama over and over again, we need to remind ourselves that we are the one consistent entity that exists in all our life episodes. The good news is we have the means to break an unproductive cycle any time we want. *"Putting a Soul spin on things."*

$\mathcal{I}$t's true we should love ourselves as we are at every stage of our growth and journey, but it also makes sense to want to reach our full potential. *"I choose to be all I am created to be."*

$\mathcal{N}$ote to My Human Self: When it comes to anxiety, anger, and fear—emotions that keep you from feeling happy and productive—you have an option! You can put them in a balloon and allow them to float up for the day. After all, we don't have time for negativity! We have to concentrate on getting the job done.

"Letting it all go!"

$\mathcal{S}$eek and ye shall find... So, if we choose every day to look for the beauty in people, places, and things, we will always find ourselves surrounded by beautiful people, places, and things. *"See the beauty!"*

$\mathcal{O}$ur thoughts combined with our emotions create the feelings we experience moment to moment and day by day. It stands to reason, then, if we experience uncomfortable thoughts and emotions, we have to change what is running amok in our heads and in our hearts. If negative emotions from the past keep dictating the current state of our being, healing needs to take place. If thoughts and fears of the future are determining our current state of mind, we need to manipulate them into positive statements and images that will help us achieve our goals. In order to grow forward as our best selves, we have to be *"Existing in the now with constructive thoughts and emotions."*

$\mathcal{W}$e should move forward daily with a big mindset and belief in what we can accomplish, because, after all, *our only failure would be to never try.* *"I'm doing this!"*

We don't have to deprive ourselves of anything; instead, we should just change our minds about what we want. When we decide to want what is right and good for our bodies, our lives, and those we love, we won't have to worry about being tempted by what is not good for us. We will be more inclined to make better choices, and we will find ourselves *"Feeling happy and fulfilled."*

It is not helpful to judge our past, present, or future based on how we feel at any given moment or on any given day. No mood or mindset should define our entire lives! When stress gets to us— whether it is from doubt and fear about the future, anger and resentment about our past, or confusion about where we are now—we can ask for guidance. This request immediately clears our minds and allows for internal wisdom to be revealed. Ask for wisdom, and it will be given. *"Soul, please step in!"*

If others don't know what we already went through, then how could they know how far we have already come? We can choose to listen to other people's opinions of us, but we should only take heed of what will be helpful for our growth. *"Taking what I need and letting go of the rest."*

a "recall-a-holic" is what we become when we constantly repeat and replay a hurtful event in our own mind, out loud to the person who hurt us, or to anyone that will listen. In order to stop perpetuating the negative and unproductive energy this behavior creates, we will need to stop lamenting about the past and start living in the present. We should make a decision every day to move forward exerting our mental and emotional energy on what will instigate positive forward movement. *"All my words reflect the amazing future I am choosing to walk into."*

What we are capable of doing will only become apparent when we are fed up with mediocrity. *"Facing the challenge; Rising in excellence!"*

Our past is a part of us, but we are not beholden to our past. Our bodies are a part of us, but we are not beholden to our bodies. Our emotions are a part of us, but we are not beholden to any of our emotions! We have the ability to change everything that is not in alignment with a healthy state of mind and body. Our daily reminder: *"Bearing right onto the road to wellness!"*

When we get tired and frustrated and want to give up, we should choose to remember the last time we wanted to but didn't; then recall the time before that, and the time before that, and the time before that… *"I am resilient!"*

True growth and our best outcome will be realized when we overcome the discomfort we feel while trying something new. If we are not a little uncomfortable, we are probably not breaking out of the ordinary and reaching the highest level of awareness and advancement we can achieve. *"Push beyond this!"*

We were born into and raised under certain circumstances but now, as adults, we are privileged to have millions of choices we can make. Those new decisions—not our past ones—are what determine our future and destiny. If we keep blaming ourselves or others for where we have ended up, we will continue to stay exactly where we are. Instead, we should consider everything that happened to us *back then* to have been a necessary step to get to *here*. *"Stepping into my fresh, new, amazing day!"*

Question: How long does it take for a negative thought to change into a positive one? Answer: As long as we let it take! Remember to *"Manipulate it!"*

The next time we woefully ask ourselves, how we ended up here, let's remember, we haven't 'ended up' just yet. Until our bodies leave this planet, our lives will always be on their way to somewhere. *"Stepping into the future I've been preparing for."*

Life without love is like breathing without oxygen. *"Love deeply today."*

No need to muscle it! The more human force we exert, the less our spiritual power can engage. *"Flowing with the power of my Soul!"*

Criticism can never be truly constructive! If we have to criticize in order to counsel or offer an opinion, it means we haven't found the right words. We need to lovingly construct thoughts before we speak them because when we do, we build relationships that are truly wonderful. *"Building up with loving words."*

Settling for less and wishing for more is giving us more of the less and less of the more! Instead of an imbalanced and unfair energetic exchange, we need to exert ourselves by saying, *"I am worthy to receive."*

P*erfect Love* is soulful love that when committed to will become more powerful than any human weakness a relationship can experience. It is love in perfection that can right the wrongs in imperfect people. Today, think about *"Committing to perfect love."*

Dandelions might be considered an unwelcome weed in any lawn or garden, but they are really beautiful and important flowers. Their pollen supports our bee population, and their leaves offer us a slightly bitter but nutritious salad. The same can be said of some people in our lives... the ones we just don't like and may want to rid ourselves of. Even if we manage to weed some of them out, more will eventually start popping up. When we decide to view these people as important and essential creations of this planet, then their contribution to our lives will finally be recognized. *"Love them as they are; Love them anyway."*

We don't need to be smarter, more talented, or richer than we are right now to get what we want. We do, however, need to rid ourselves of any such doubt or fear before we can take advantage of our innate abilities and co-creation tools. Repeat: *"I have faith in the Powers that be; I believe in me!"*

While judging others, we waste an awful lot of time and energy we could be using to eradicate issues within ourselves. When someone irritates or triggers us, we should reflect on it by asking ourselves this very tough question, "Is what I am seeing in this person supposed to be mirrored back to me?" At that moment we will become open to hearing our own truth; potentially, what we may need to change about ourselves. No matter how harsh this practice may seem on our persona, doing so will always lead to tremendous growth and forward movement. Remember: *"Everyone can be my messenger; everyone can be my teacher."*

It can be said that sports and exercise are like Feng Shui for the mind and body: The more worthwhile physical energy we generate, the more endorphins will be released and the easier it will be to stay balanced and centered.

"A body in positive motion
tends to stay in positive Emotion."

$\mathcal{D}$oes a daisy ever try to be a rose? Since each of us is special in our own right, why would we ever waste energy and time wanting or trying to be like anyone else? To grow forward as our best selves in our own truth, strength, and light, we need to live authentically right now. No matter who we think we were yesterday or want to be tomorrow, let's be okay with the person we are today! *"Embracing all of who I am and all of who I am preparing to be!"*

$\mathcal{D}$enial is a terrible thing to waste, and we should be excited to address what we may be in denial of even if fear is preventing us from revealing some truth. With ears tuned in and eyes focused, announce, *"Show me what I am afraid to see and hear, and even if I resist, help me through it."*

$\mathcal{L}$iving life without purpose is like climbing a staircase that leads to nowhere. We can keep going up but will that effort ever take us where we want to go? Instead, let's declare our positive intentions and help make each moment and movement of our day bring us toward our goal. Whether it is a minute of deep breathing or an hour of hard work, imagine *"Each step I climb is worthy of my time!"*

Science says that we are always more clear-headed and energetically powerful when we are connected to nature. So today, find a garden to sit in, a tree to stand under, an ocean to wade in; even a grass patch will do. Then, while bare-footed, connect with the ground and repeat, *"Earth, energize me!"*

If we ignore what our bodies are trying to tell us they want and need from us, then we shouldn't be surprised when they stop listening to what we want and need from them. We can decide now to start listening to signs and symptoms and then ask, *"What do I need for ultimate health and wellness?"*

The only thing we should ever regret in our lives is any time we spend regretting something in our lives! Every hardship gives us the opportunity to rise up; every past event has the potential to help us grow forward. *"Grateful for every experience."*

Can I? Should I? Could I? We can't keep letting question marks keep us from making exclamation points! Taking the plunge becomes easier when we realize that the only failure is to never try. *"Yes, I can!"*

Our bodies are our judge and jury, and whatever we put in them can be used for or against us. We have to keep ourselves free of pollutants by choosing foods and drinks that keep us healthy, well-balanced, and empowered. ***"Everything I put in me helps me to thrive!"***

When we find ourselves in the company of someone who is angry or bitter, we don't have to allow that energy to affect us. We need to remember that we have just as much potential to help them change their mood as they do ours. Hold onto this knowingness: ***"Love and compassion will always overpower anger and bitterness."***

We decide the *kind* of person we want to be. Ask, "Do I want to hurt someone today or help? Take or share? Criticize and belittle or uplift and inspire? Do I want to hold a grudge forever or start to forgive?" Considering we deserve to get back exactly what we give out, it makes sense to ***"Be kind!"***

Someone else's perception of us is their reality, and we may have to deal with their reality, but we don't have to own it! Repeat: ***"I am the only one who can define Me."***

When we continually talk about the should-haves, would-haves, and could-haves in our lives, we won't get the chance to say, "I did, I saw, I conquered!" Today we can change that by writing our goals and stating our motives so clearly that nothing can stand in our way, not even ourselves. *"My needs are met; my goals are set; I'm a body in motion."*

What we feel, think, and believe creates energy that actually emanates from us and is then shared with everyone we come in contact with. To put our best self forward, we need to demand of ourselves every day to be *"Thinking, feeling, and exuding positive energy."*

Everyone falls from grace once in a while. So if we want others to give us the benefit of the doubt, we have to give them the benefit of the doubt as well. Today, as a practice, no matter what people say or do, opt for a tolerant attitude. After all, we are all human beings doing the best we can do with what we have to work with. *"Tolerance is mine."*

What we aren't doing and what we don't even know we can do… that's the biggest part of who we are! Declare: *"I am stepping into my life on purpose today, reaching my full potential!"*

Adopt a wait-and-see attitude and expect a come-what-may outcome. Instead of allowing for 'whatever' to transpire in a day, though, we should remember how much spiritual power we are actually carrying with us on our daily journey. Walking into a productive day is easy when we clearly defining where we want to go and what we want to accomplish. Then, we should expect to intuitively hear each step we need to take. When we tune in and declare, we'll always find our way there. *"Wisely productive!"*

A person who consistently judges, blames, criticizes, insults and demoralizes others should have our compassion, but not our attention. It would behoove us to disengage from negative dialogue and demand of ourselves to *"Seek and speak goodness."*

Worthiness is based on willingness so if we are willing to do what it takes to live our best and most beautiful life, we are worthy of having our best, most beautiful life. *"I am willing; I am worthy!"*

*L*ove is a language we all used and understood before we ever heard, spoke, or understood a single word. No matter what hurt, harm, or 'hard knocks' we have experienced, we need to remember that our innate wisdom about love never left us. Repeat often: *"I am Love personified."*

*W*hether it is their issue, ours, or a little of both, when we find ourselves spinning in a useless drama cycle with someone—and we want to stop the cycle—we would first need to take personal responsibility for our participation in it. If that doesn't get us out of hot water, then make good use of it! Wash away blame with unconditional love and rinse off any remaining anger and resentment with love and tolerance. That is the only way to truly become *"Clean and Clear of it!"*

*A*nger, resentment, and *un*forgiveness exist in society. They are prevalent emotions; sometimes in ourselves, sometimes in others. Occasionally the negative energy these emotions create can feel strong enough to blow us away, but that's only because we haven't poured enough goodness on them. Remember, *"No amount of hate has the strength to overpower love."*

It is our right to respond to people and situations as we see fit, but there is only one right way to act and be that will actually help make all our situations and relationships become better. *"Showing the best of who I am."*

Life doesn't just happen to us. Our free will dictates how our lives will unfold. Each day we need to specifically announce our will through powerful statements about what we want to achieve and where we want to go. Our proclamations will automatically bring to light the best paths and directions we can take to reach those goals. *"Always willing my highest good into existence."*

Mental and emotional distress can lead to physical disease, but we don't have to let that happen. Mentally speaking, we are not beholden to negative feelings. They don't have to 'own' us, but we do need to own up to them. When we set our intention to reach harmony in our mind, body, and soul, then the root causes of our negativity will be revealed to us. After we accept what needs to change, we can request healing, and the subsequent steps we need to take will become obvious. *"Achieving Harmony!"*

*N*ote to My Ego Self: There will be days ahead when you truly confuse me… when you make it hard for me to see where I need to go and how things ought to be. These are the days I'm going to need your support, but you will just keep getting in my way. Guess what… today is one of those days! So, I've decided to gently and lovingly tell you to ***"Go take a hike!" You really need to get some clarity."***

We don't have to worry about what we don't know. Instead, we need to be committed to moving forward doing the best we can with what we do know. Then, as we move forward through each day, expect that *"Whatever is needed will present itself."*

When we listen with only our heads, what we hear forms an opinion. When we listen with only our hearts, what we hear instigates an emotion. When we use only our gut instincts to interpret a situation, we sense it as good or bad or right or wrong. However, when we engage all three of our gifts—our heads' intelligence, our hearts' ability to love, and our guts' innate instincts—we are immediately *"Gleaning truth, feeling compassion, and moving forward with complete understanding."*

It is important to remember: We don't have to know how to get to our best life; we just have to want it, keep willing it, and believe we are worthy of having it, and the magnificent and comprehensive energy we were created with will take over from there. *"Living my best day today."*

We don't have to take offense to an offensive statement. Instead, we can choose to use a negative remark to seek some truth about our own energy, our current circumstance, or our relationship with the person making the statement. When we choose to take the good out of the not so good, we turn a perceived negative into a positive. *"I am always better off knowing the truth."*

If the chemicals in one tiny aspirin can rid us of a headache, then what is to say that all the chemicals in every plate and cup of food and drink we consume aren't giving us that headache in the first place? Our ailments and symptoms are signals that our bodies are in some sort of distress, and food is a known culprit—known to experts as far back as Hippocrates. He also told us to "let food be thy medicine," so today, let's try *"Eating and drinking what is needed for optimum health and wellness."*

It is normal for us to have doubts and fears, but we can choose to move beyond any and all human frailties, any and all minutes of our day, when we say, *"Right now, I'm tapping into Soul power!"*

The second we drop our human need to judge or categorize something or someone as "good" or "bad," we receive the soulful insight to help us heal, teach, lead, speak up, shut up, or leave the situation alone. Discernment is our gift, but we only get to use that gift when we close our minds to judgment and allow our Souls to *"Bring some love into it."*

A note from me, your Soul: No matter what you think you lack in IQ, you were born with the ability to interpret profound concepts. No matter what you think you lack in talent, you are inordinately gifted. No matter how imperfect you think you have acted on occasion, you were made perfectly. So you can't really use the fact that you are 'only human' as an excuse to not live up to your human potential! I am here to remind you today and every day, that you are *"More than qualified."*

Nothing we have ever been through in the past has been a waste of our time! All of it has added up to the sum of who we are at this very moment, and that means we are in a perfect position right now to *"Live this new day in a profound and powerful way."*

We can't expect to be happy and productive people if we are living in unhealthy and deprived bodies. Today, we can make the commitment to start *"Taking care of the vessel that houses me."*

Higher education and knowledge can be powerful tools but unfortunately, they don't always equate to higher knowing and definitive truth. If they did, everyone would always be in agreement about everything! Until the complete truth about all that exists in this world and our universe is revealed, we should surrender our educated guesses and opinions in favor of love and compassion. Both will help us see and hear more truth; both will help us work better together so we can make sense of what we don't yet understand. *"More tolerance; more love; more truth."*

No matter how down we may feel at any given moment, we have the ability to lift ourselves up. We are all-inclusive, co-creating, self-motivating machines, and when we decide to rise, we will rise! *"Opening my eyes and ears to the possibilities!"*

Our human selves don't necessarily know the right paths to take, but there is a part of us that always knows how to reach our full potential. Every step we take can be purpose-driven or ego-driven; it's our choice to make. Be on the Soul's path, *"On a journey of great discovery and joy."*

Experts in psychology tell us that we shouldn't judge our feelings as right or wrong, but isn't it a good idea to question whether they are real? Sometimes our biochemistry, the weather, an illness, the food and drink we consume, our environment, and even a past trauma will trick and then trap us into a compromising mood. Instead of realizing that, though, we often try to find something or someone to blame for the way we feel. So whether right, wrong, real or imagined, we need to make a request daily to, not only see clearly, but to *feel clearly* because discovering the origin of our unproductive emotions may eventually set us free of them. Ask, *"Why am I feeling this way?"*

People who respect themselves and have love in their lives don't trash other people. They have no desire to rubberneck on someone else's journey because they are too busy and delighted traveling on their own. *"Loving where I am heading."*

We have the ability to see and hear all sides of an issue. Everyone we encounter and every important issue we are faced with deserves this clarity. It is likely, though, that our minds won't allow us to hear the truth unless we bring our Souls into the conversation. Decide: *"It is better to do right than it is to be right."*

It is our responsibility to hold true to who we are irrespective of the emotional or mental pain someone else may be trying to inflict on us. No one can push us out of a loving state of being if we don't allow it. Stand strong, *"Remaining in a space of love and goodness."*

No matter where we are, who we are with, or what we are doing, we can still be on a spiritual journey, moving in the direction of love, power, and grace. Once we make the decision to be all we are meant to be, nothing—not even the weaker part of ourselves—can stop us. *"Growing forward today."*

Be amazed by nature because the more beauty we find in our surroundings, the more beauty we see in our lives. *"Seeing the beauty; feeling the joy!"*

We cannot expect anyone to love us more than we are willing to love ourselves. We cannot expect anyone to respect us more than we are willing to respect ourselves. We cannot expect anyone to have more confidence in us than we have in ourselves! Today, repeat, *"I love, respect, and believe in Me."*

If we want a great partner in life, we need to be a great partner in life: We need to be as loving toward another as we want them to be toward us; we need to share as much of ourselves as we want another to share. Reciprocity in love does exist, but only if we are willing to give out what we want to receive. *"Giving and receiving love."*

Each of us possesses the mental and emotional tools needed to successfully handle and produce everything we need and want, but sometimes we need to be reminded of that. In order to succeed, we need to take ourselves out of survival mode and into thrival mode. *"Thriving through today!"*

Life doesn't just happen; we walk down the paths our minds (thoughts) and hearts (emotions) bring into existence. Our feelings have the ability to create our best future or to prevent us from realizing it. So, it's important to remain mentally and emotionally clear about what we want. Today, expect to *"Walk into the future I have prepared for."*

If we were to enter into an argument intending to see and hear the truth, to offer our understanding, and to propose a mutually satisfying outcome, then the argument has already ended! It doesn't have to be him or her, them or me. *"It can always be We."*

Our Souls are like the sun... No matter the storms endured, they always remain steadfast; they are always able to offer light; they're always willing to lead us into a bright new day. Unlike the sun, though, we have to ask our Souls to rise in us each day. And when we do, we bask in that love and shine with that light. *"Rise Soul ... Rise!"*

If we keep our thoughts focused on the past, we won't ever be able to enjoy the present, nor will we be able to envision any good stuff for the future. Today *"Choose and use thoughts wisely."*

Building walls around our hearts will work well to keep the hurt out, but that habit also keeps the love from coming in. Being afraid and closed off makes us weak, while love and vulnerability create great strength. So loving more—not less—keeps us protected. Envision *"Love flowing in; Love flowing out."*

Going from "Woe is me" to, "Whoa! It's me!"… *That* is when intentional manifestation all begins. It is always best to take full responsibility for a situation we find ourselves in as it is the only way we will be able to take control of its outcome. Create positive change going forward by asking, *"What is my role in this?"*

Until we change the view we have of ourselves through our own eyes, we will never change how the rest of the world views us through theirs. Look in the mirror and start *"Seeing greatness."*

We don't have to categorize the direction we are headed in as right or wrong, good or bad. Instead, we can just ask ourselves if the path we are on is getting us where we want to go. *"All the paths I tread upon lead to more success and happiness."*

Imagine if we lived no-excuse lives... what would life be like? Actually, there's no need to wonder. We can always choose to step into our daily life with a no-excuse, no-limits, no-boundaries, no-holding-back attitude. *"Stepping into my life on purpose today!"*

We won't be able to fill up with powerful and worthy thoughts and emotions unless we are first willing to get rid of weak and unhealthy ones. We need to empty out all unnecessary feelings in order to move forward powerfully with love and grace. *"Cleaning my heart; clearing my head."*

Being a person who can inflate people's spirit or deflate them... we get to decide. And if we can't think of a way to make a comment uplifting, encouraging, authentic, viable, and constructive, we can choose to hold back until the wiser and more loving part of ourselves can pick the right words and sentiments. Remember, *"When I help others rise, I rise with them."*

Our bodies are our Earth vehicles; our Souls are our navigation system; our minds plug in the destination, and our hearts pump the fuel. Ready, set, *"Going to where my dreams live!"*

$\mathcal{T}$oday, when something we think about doesn't make us feel good or strong or outstanding, we can choose to *"Positively manipulate it!"*

$\mathcal{W}$hen we allow fear, anxiety, anger, or uncertainty to dictate each step we take, it puts us in an endless maze of confusion. We don't have to stay there, though! We can go from a maze to *amazing* anytime we want by reversing our negative state of mind. *"Paving a new path to power!"*

$\mathcal{W}$e are born and exist in human bodies which are influenced by everything we put inside and everything existing outside. We all have human egos that are inherently self-serving. We come from pasts that can influence our current perception and reality. But even with all of this possibly working against us, we can still love ourselves exactly the way we are at this very moment. And because everyone else subsists each day under the same circumstances, we should allow for their humanness as well. It is important for us to remember: We are all journeying together; we all have Souls willing us to rise and do better today than we did the day before. Sometimes we follow that will; sometimes we don't. *"Forgiving myself for being human; forgiving others for being the same."*

$\mathcal{W}$e walk into the future that our thoughts highlight for us. A simple way to explain this is to picture ourselves wearing a helmet with a powerful flashlight attached. When we think doubtful, resistant thoughts, our heads turn in that direction, lighting up the path that will take us to that negative place. When we think positive and powerful thoughts, our heads turn to light up the path that leads to empowerment. Since we are all walking into some kind of future every minute of every day, it makes sense to be aware of the paths we are illuminating. *"Always mindful of where I am heading."*

We don't have to run away from negative emotions; we can heal from them. We don't have to sit with negative thoughts; we can manipulate out of them. We don't have to wait for life to happen *to* us; we can make it happen *for* us! When it comes to thoughts and emotions, *"Whether I decide to heal, manipulate, or let them go, I am always able to take control!"*

The hurt and pain we sometimes find ourselves stuck in can be seen as a sword embedded in our heart, constantly piercing and twisting our perception and keeping us grounded to the past and the people and situations that pained us. We can choose at any time to allow that sword a way through; and when we do, the healing begins. This visual therapy, along with a willingness to forgive, can liberate a troubled heart and help it start to mend. *"Allowing the sword to pass through me. Letting the healing begin."*

Living with positive intention and true purpose doesn't make life harder; it makes life easier! And to get started each and every day, we need to say, *"Ready, willing, and able to be the best that I can be."*

True happiness can be achieved when we get out of our doubtful and judgmental minds and choose to perceive everything with the help of our hearts. *"Loving and appreciating this moment."*

People who ignore or reject our gifts and talents have no idea what they are missing out on. Lucky for us, there are so many who will appreciate what we have to offer. *"Attracting like-minded and appreciative people."*

Always and never: When it comes to describing other peoples' behavior, let us assume; there is never a time when 'always' fits, and there is always a time to choose a better word than 'never.' *"When I seek the goodness, I will see the goodness."*

*T*oday, let's start our day like a racehorse by bursting through the gate and hurling our bodies onto the track. Let's run with the wind blowing through our hair and dirt scattering beneath our feet. Let's enjoy every minute doing exactly what we were born to do. Repeat: ***"I am a champion!"***

*W*e are, each and every one of us, very special but how many of us believe it? We are inordinately gifted but are we all using the gifts we were given? We are individual and unique, but do we often follow rather than lead? Are we living each day allowing ourselves to reach higher, dig deeper, and expand beyond the ordinary? When we answer with a 'no' to these questions, then we are not living up to our potential. We are instead, 'existing in the consequential' by actually waiting for each minute to unfold. Today, we can change all that! ***"I am aspiring to be all that I am here to be."***

*I*n case some 'F-words' are needed today, here are a few to choose from: Faithful, Fearless, Fortitude, Flow, Forgiveness, Freedom, Fulfillment, Fun, Fantasy, Family, Fantastic… Willfully choose to ***"Use all positive F-words today!"***

𝕴nstead of not feeling good about our bodies, we can decide to use our bodies to start feeling good about ourselves! Walking is a *good* start. ***"Stepping with positive energy today!"***

𝖂e are energetic beings that are continually being affected by all that we are thinking and feeling. So right now and at this very moment, we need to ask ourselves if we are happy and excited about what we are thinking and feeling. If not, let's change both. Let's fill our heads and hearts with the same positive energy we want flowing back to us. ***"Happiness is a choice; I'm choosing happiness."***

𝕴f we keep saying we will do something after this or that, then we need to realize that there will always be another this or that, but this moment will never come back. There may never be a better time than *now*. ***"It is time to start."***

𝕿oday is a great day to experience great things! ***"My list of great things:***

_____

_____

_____

_____

We can't keep saying *they* have to do it. We can't expect others to do what we may not be willing to do. Truth be told, what we think our country needs to do as a nation is what we need to start doing as individuals.

> *"I am willing to walk the talk and be the change I want to see in my world."*

We don't have to look very far for the reasons we feel imbalanced, uneasy, and not in alignment with our desires. The answers are found here—in our current state of mind and being and in what we are experiencing at this moment. We need to ask ourselves, "Am I imagining what I want or what I don't want? Am I envisioning where I want to go or where I don't want to go?" Our 'now' moment is all we need to change every moment thereafter. Repeat: *"I am balanced, at peace, and in alignment with my goals."*

Instead of allowing our heads to sit in a quandary, we can attempt to seek out a solution. Q & A Meditation allows us to ask a Question of our Soul (and/or Higher Power) and then wait expectedly for the Answer. It is important to note, though, that we have to be ready, willing, and able to accept what is being offered for our consideration. If we are too afraid of what we might see or hear, we need to be willing to push beyond any discomfort we find ourselves in. To do that, we need to announce: *"I'm willfully uncovering my ears and opening my eyes; seeing and hearing what there is to know!"*

When we start to complain about the way our bodies feel, it means our bodies have already been complaining to us! Every symptom, ache, pain, weight loss, or gain—even fatigue and lack of focus —they are all distress calls, and we need to take these calls seriously. Today, ask to become aware; choose to know the root cause of all health concerns. *"Taking heed of my body's needs."*

Having lived life up until this moment, we can realize how often we have learned and loved and lost. Now though, moving forward, we can admit to ourselves: "If I love a lot more while I'm living, I will have to lose and learn a lot less!" *"Loving more every day."*

Guilt is a useless sentiment unless we use it to *not* do something we might regret. After the fact, it can't bring any goodness to anyone—not ourselves, and not the people or circumstances we feel guilty about. Instead, we can choose to manipulate that guilt energy into useful service and atonement. From this moment forward, *"I am influencing lives in a profound and beautiful way!"*

"Knowing brings power and strength, making denial no longer necessary."

A great life will not fall from the sky. We cannot win it, nor will it ever be granted to us without us being willing to do what it takes to achieve it. Living life beautifully is a decision we need to make every day and sometimes more than once in a day. *"Spending my time creating the life I truly want."*

Self-esteem is what we think of ourselves. Self-love is how we feel about ourselves. Self-worth is what we allow for ourselves. If our past left us low in any or all three, we should realize we don't need to repeat history. We get to define who we are and who we will be. Repeat: *"My New Day; My New Life Story!"*

Without truth there is no trust; without integrity, there is no honesty. Lack of respect means lack of honor, and no love means no forgiveness. Whatever we want to receive from others, we need to do unto them. *"Willfully choosing to share love, respect, honor, and truth."*

Taking responsibility isn't about laying fault or blame; it is about understanding our participation in all our life circumstances. We should be happy to take responsibility because doing so offers us the ability to co-create the life we want. *"I choose to know how I got to HERE."*

When a decision of what to do or which way to go does not bring us inner peace, we need to remember that we have another choice: We can make the decision to make *no* decision until we have more information or feel more comfortable. Ask for direction, remain open to discovery, and believe that, *"As all there is to know presents itself, the best choice will be obvious."*

Note to My Human Self: So you have issues; just love yourself anyway. So you screwed up; just love yourself anyway! So you sometimes do and say stupid things; just *"LOVE YOURSELF ANYWAY!"*

"Am I stuck?" When we honestly assess our state of being, we can move forward and in the direction we are preparing for. To open ourselves to a beautiful and bright new future, we have to admit to the block, then repeat, *"Pushing past this!"*

We are like mental and emotional magnets that pull in, walk into, and attach ourselves to the people and circumstances that match the energy we are generating. So if we want abundance, clarity, health, and wealth, we have to switch out of the energy of want, need, helplessness, and lack. The fastest way to do that is to have gratitude! Being in a state of happiness and thankfulness for what we do have, immediately sets ourselves up to bring in more of what we want. We can be a grumpy magnet or a happy magnet; a woe magnet or a wow magnet... It's always our choice what state of mind and being we exist in. *"Aware of all that I have to feel happy about."*

When it comes to being human, there is no such thing as 'damaged goods,' but we should consider a state of being called 'as is.' Life has gotten each of us *here*, and here is where we should choose to heal every aspect of ourselves that is preventing us from living authentically. Let's be grateful for every crack and chip, then choose love and forgiveness to repair them. Believe: ***"I am newly restored!"***

We might think anger creates a great shield against any further pain someone might cause us, but the only thing our anger blocks is self-growth. We shouldn't feel guilty about that, though. Anger in the form of righteousness can be helpful when we need the strength to stand up for what is right and good. Prolonged anger, intolerance, and *un*forgiveness, however, will do nothing except attract more of the same into our lives. Staying in that state of mind and heart leaves us unable to bring in inspiring thoughts and healing emotions. When needing to protect ourselves, we can declare: ***"Love is the only sovereignty worth pursuing; the only shield worth wearing."***

It is hard to give up the foods and drinks we enjoy, but let's admit that it's harder to be tired, ailing, sick, addicted, aimless, or confused! We need to keep ourselves nourished with what our bodies need, not necessarily what we want to give them. We also have to start looking at healthy options as delicious and satisfying. To reinforce our decision to make healthy choices, let's remember that we'll never have a clear head and healthy life without having a clean diet and healthy body. *"Filling up with the good stuff!"*

When we find ourselves 'going with the flow,' let's consider whose flow it is: ours or everyone else's. Today, repeat: *"Honoring my flow and my beautiful goal."*

Being in a humble state of mind means we don't ever have to worry about not being smart enough. Wisdom will always find its way into our heads when we recognize that, humanly speaking, we don't know everything. *"Eager to learn."*

The ultimate warrior pose: Place the right leg forward and bent at the knee. Keep the left leg behind and straight. Hold the left arm and hand behind the body with palm facing toward the ground. The right arm and hand extend out in front (directly over the front leg) with its palm facing up and lifted toward the sky. Now, allow for powerful, light energy to surge down through the right hand as the Earth's energy comes up through the left.

"Physically grounded; spiritually lifted and ready for anything today!"

We have been taught to not compare ourselves with others, but sometimes doing that can be helpful. When we think we can't do something, we can recall the man with no arms that plays the guitar with his feet. When we become lost in self-pity, we should remember the injured soldier who went back to fight for his country with a prosthetic leg. When we feel overcome by sorrow, let us realize the number of people who tragically lost loved ones and went on to turn their pain into a gain for humanity. The truth is we are all special but pain and discomfort are not. The way we handle our painful circumstances will determine the life we are going to lead and the strength we gain from having gone through them. Our Souls, they are always prompting us to *"Heal and rise up again!"*

We can *prevent* a quarrel with love more effectively than we can fight one with hate. *"Love really does conquer all."*

No matter where we are heading, if we are coming from love, it is bound to be a successful journey. *"Choosing love always leads to a successful outcome."*

$\mathcal{M}$ost people would agree that our Soul selves are powerful, unconditional, and able to guide, comfort, heal, and love our human selves. No matter how closed off and effaced from that inner strength we become, it is never closed off from us. To turn back toward awareness, comfort, and power, we only have to believe it exists. Ask, listen, and have faith that *"There is more to* Me *than just* Me.*"*

$\mathcal{W}$hen we decide to be the best we can be, we create spiritual energy that radiates inside and outside of ourselves. This energy is what keeps us moving poignantly toward our goals. None of us needs to know how to get to our best life, persona, relationship, job, or body. We just have to want it, believe we are worthy of having it, and then expect to spend each minute of our day achieving it. *"Living as if I am already there."*

$\mathcal{W}$e need to try and laugh at ourselves and our human antics a little each day, which shouldn't be that hard considering how human we really are. *"Finding the humor in being me."*

*T*oday let's be amazed and amused by simple pleasures as we look at all aspects of our lives with new appreciation. Sometimes being 'small-minded' is the best thing we can do for ourselves and those around us. *"Appreciating the little things."*

*A*n intense feeling we are experiencing may not be caused by our present circumstances. We can get to the root of our emotions and thoughts by asking ourselves, "Is this feeling stemming from this current situation, or is it coming from some time ago?" Doing this exercise will help us move forward with clarity. *"Healing from my past; excited about my future; making the most of this day."*

*Y*es, there is strength in numbers, but when in doubt that each of us can't *single-heartedly* have a positive impact on this world, let's remember: *"One is a number too!"*

We should always strive to love others unconditionally no matter what negative state of being we think they are in because, most likely, they are trapped and unable to recognize or hear their own Soul. It doesn't make sense to be angry or hateful toward anyone sitting in their own darkness. It is within our power to love others, or at a minimum to be tolerant of them through their frailties, and with that, we generate healing energy for them, as well as peace within ourselves. Choose to always *"Be the light others can follow."*

As far as betrayal is concerned, we need to remind ourselves that we can't change another person, but we can forgive them for being so human. Then we can turn our minds and energy away from the hurtful act and put our focus on restoration for ourselves. When we do this, a new direction will be revealed and our life will become what we want it to be. *"Restoring; healing; lifting!"*

The moment we ask ourselves to acknowledge our participation in a life episode, we change the dynamics of that life episode. No one can ever simultaneously be a victim and a victor. *"I choose victory!"*

The first time the intern cut into a patient's body, he came to the operating table already a surgeon. The first case an attorney took on, she walked into the courtroom already a litigator. Before the sales associate attempted to sell his first car, he was a salesperson. And the author… she was a writer as soon as she typed her first word. So we shouldn't worry about never having done what we want to do. Believe, *"I am what I claim to be, and I'm setting out to do it!"*

Understand that there is no need to stop soulfully loving a person we want to detach from. We can decide to sever any negative earthly bond that exists between ourselves and another but still choose to stay lovingly and soulfully connected to them. Doing so will allow us to move forward on our own, in our best light, and at full strength and speed. *"Cutting this earthly bond between myself and _____."*

Note to My Ego Self: You think you have it tough? Get over yourself! Remember, when you're whining, you're not shining! *"Shining my way through today."*

There is no better time than now to set our minds straight on this one fact: Each and every one of us has all the tools, qualities, and potential we need to make our lives wonderful. When we fall prey to our doubts, we need to overcome them by repeating: *"All I need to succeed is always available to me."*

If we allow ourselves to dwell in anger and *un*forgiveness, we bring in more anger and *un*forgiveness. If we dwell in love, we bring in more love; stay in hope and faith and get more of the same. Emotions and thoughts create an energy that is returned to us, so why would we want to discharge anything that isn't, at the very least, helpful to ourselves and others? Today, willfully choose to *"Exude beautiful energy!"*

Oil and vinegar; peanut butter and jelly; ice cream and nuts… sometimes what is so different can come together to make something very special. We can and should allow everyone to shine in their own special way so when we stand side by side, all sorts of combinations of power and potential will be realized. Today let's *"Honor the uniqueness in others."*

There are four prerequisites needed to obtain something that we want: (1) The creation of a goal with a beautiful motive attached, (2) Belief and faith in our ability to achieve it, (3) Willingness to do the work to get it, and (4) Worthiness to receive it. Understand that without the fourth prerequisite, we could be standing right next to what we have envisioned and worked so hard for, but never see it, know it, or accept it as our own. Believe and repeat: *"My willingness proves my worthiness!"*

We don't have to wait until the new year to make a resolution to change something in our lives. We can start fresh *anytime* we want! *"Today is Anew day."*

Over a lifetime, we have collected everything from a traumatic moment to a fond memory; an old, outdated belief system to an intelligent perspective; some super trivial nonsense all the way to super wisdom. Let's take a moment to acknowledge who we want to be: hoarders and negativity reapers or releasers who understand which moments are keepers? It is time to concentrate on *"Letting go of what no longer serves me."*

*"See Love, hear Love, speak Love,
and there is no evil."*

We are powerful beings who will walk toward and bring into our lives what we mentally and emotionally put out for consideration. Only the best feelings will generate the best circumstances, so *"Build forth with a positive thought."*

Note to My Human Self: You can walk into any life path you choose. What do you want to accomplish? Where do you want to go? Who do you want to be? What are you waiting for? Write it all down and then repeat: *"I am mindful of who I am and where I am going!"*

Deciding to forgive means we will no longer be attached to incidents we want to forget. Deciding to eat healthy means we won't have to drag our bodies through so many hours of our day. Deciding to appreciate what we have means that our minds and hearts will be filled with gratitude instead of regret. Everything we do for our well being leads to a better life. *"I'm 'well' on my way today!"*

Since we will never get the chance to live this particular day again, choose to *"Take advantage of every minute that this day offers!"*

When we encounter someone who is acting out in a negative way, we can decide to separate the act from the person. We can choose to see the Soul in them no matter how much darkness is blocking our view. *"Seeing their Soul; bringing them light."*

What if our heads were consistently guided by INSPIRATION—powerful thoughts that transcend our own human needs and wants to suggest we do what is right and good for the whole? What if our hearts were ASPIRING to love unconditionally and boundlessly with ultimate forgiveness? What if our instinctual selves had the MOTIVATION and drive to consistently strive to be the best we can be? What would our lives be like? Let's find out! *"I.A.M. is fully engaged!"*

We should accept the understanding that we have emotional triggers, but we shouldn't accept having to live with them for the rest of our lives! Search out the cause of each trigger, then *"Heal and release it."*

Each and every day presents itself as an opportunity to expand our horizons. So, refuse to grow old. Instead, *"Grow potential!"*

We should choose forgiveness for our own peace of mind and for all the people in our lives who deserve to have us whole, at full strength, and healed. Forgiveness is a gift we give to ourselves which everyone we love will also receive. Acknowledge and then repeat: *"How can I ever be the best I can be if I forever believe that someone has already gotten the best of me?"*

Even when clouds fill the sky, the sun is still radiating behind them, and so is the light that shines within us. No matter what seemingly negative experience we may face; no matter how dim things may seem to get, our Souls will always help us *"Shine through today!"*

This is a New Day and a fresh start, but yesterday, even if it proved difficult, may still have something to offer. We should always take the best of what we have experienced and use it to grow and learn. *"I've grown through all of my yesterdays!"*

If worthiness is measured by willingness, then be fearlessly willing to give unconditional and boundless love today. Remember: As we give unto others, we automatically become worthy of receiving the same. *"Emboldened and boundless."*

Before we get angry at someone or hold a grudge, we should try to see them as the child they once were—an infant; pure, perfect, and beaming with love. With compassion we can imagine their life and all the pain and brokenness they must have experienced to get them to where they are now. We can pray or meditate on whether we should offer them help because, realistically, when we stop being their judge, we can see and hear ways to *"Be their light."*

Should we spend our time just living, or should we decide right now to fully live every minute in the time we have been given? *"Thriving through each and every moment today!"*

Life is a full mind, body, and spirit workout that allows us to continually expand our awareness while we increase spiritual strength. Repeat: *"I always carry power and potential with me wherever I am and wherever I go."*

Let's decide to not allow our simply human selves to dictate which direction we are heading in today. Lovingly let go of ego and keep things *"Running on Soul-Power."*

$\mathcal{A}$s we stand tall in our energy space with a sword of truth in one hand and a shield of love in the other, we can rest assured we are armed with and by the greatest forms of protection that exist. Stand tall and repeat: *"It's not a challenge; it's an opportunity to succeed!"*

$\mathcal{B}$ased on years of trial and error, agony and triumph, observation and experience, let's realize that we have come through much and are still here to talk about it. We are still capable of self-growth and self-actualization. We have picked ourselves up again and again, and yet we are still ready, willing, and able to keep going. That has to mean that we are awesome, resilient beings who are *"Always rejuvenating, refreshing, and restoring!"*

$\mathcal{S}$imply put, there are no circumstances that can keep us from greatness; there are only excuses. Repeat: *"I choose to live a no-excuse life!"*

$\mathcal{W}$hat we say and do will boomerang, so decide every day to *"Make every outgoing word and action into something worthy of being returned."*

$\mathcal{E}$very time words leave of our mouths, we are either giving testimony to our inner strength or our inner struggle. *"Speak strength today."*

$\mathcal{W}$hen we bear witness or are involved in a harmful act played out by a person we at one time believed in, we can choose to forgive and perhaps decide to love them more. The truth is, when someone is not in touch with their own Soul, it's not only uncomfortable for us, it is most likely unbearable for them. *"Love them through it."*

$\mathcal{B}$uilding someone up with constructive opinion versus tearing them down with destructive criticism: It's all in the way we decide to swing that hammer. *"Building beautiful relationships today."*

$\mathcal{T}$here is no job too big; there is only ambition that is too small. Repeat: *"I believe in my ability to succeed!"*

When we label others by placing them into a category, we limit them, and when we judge them, we limit ourselves. Judgment only allows us to see and hear with one side of our being. Let's decide to see with both eyes and hear with both ears today and, for good measure, we can throw some heartfelt compassion into the mix. *"Soulfully engaged."*

Unless we have poured love and goodness on a situation, prayed, meditated, and asked to hear the truth about our participation in it, then we haven't done all we can do to heal it! *"Open to healing solutions."*

No matter what pain, anger, anxiety, or fear we feel for any injustice we endured, we should always try to seek awareness and understanding of the situation, the other person's perspective, and the state of being they are in. It does not behoove us to remain in any emotion that leaves us less than loving, compassionate, and tolerant. *"There is always more to see."*

Repeat: *"As soon as I am willing to give the tolerance and unconditional love I'm asking to receive, then tolerance and unconditional love will be returned to me."*

*A*n opinion belongs to the person offering it and doesn't necessarily have to belong to the person receiving it. Let go of what is not worthy; *"Listen and retain what is usable."*

*I*n order to stop spinning in confusion, we need to remind ourselves that we are not reliant on just our human mind. We can lift higher than the issues we face; we can rise above and gain clarity anytime we want. *"Requesting a new perspective."*

*N*ote to My Soul: *"Today, guide me to the best paths to take, the most appropriate doors to open, and the most amazing people I can meet. Remind me, too, in case I forget, that it's you who is showing me."*

*L*ike spring, love is perennial; like spring, love can make things new over and over and over again. *"Lovingly renewing every part of Me today!"*

*R*eciprocity of energy is like a spiritual law that says we can go out and do well wherever, whenever, and for whomever, with the full expectation of receiving back from wherever, whomever, and whenever it is appropriate. *"Spreading amazing energy today!"*

Timing isn't everything. In fact, timing could be the gap we are standing in, just waiting for something to happen. It may actually denote the space we are creating between our hope and readiness. So every minute we blame timing for what we haven't been able to bring to fruition is a minute of time we just made time more important than our goals. As soon as we believe that what we want is attainable, we will remember we are journeying towards it and *"Walking right into it."*

Our Souls don't follow a calendar. We can go back and apply soulful insight just as easily as we can use it to move forward. When we choose to learn and grow from our past experiences, we are given the opportunity to rewrite a beautiful new perception of it. *"My past has taught me well!"*

If we want to change the way we feel about ourselves, we have to change our inner dialogue. Choosing only positive words, assertions, and compliments will create a new habit that will help us to restore and heal our persona. *"Positively changing my mind."*

We should selfishly and selflessly give of ourselves today because we want to; because it is what we were made to do; because it is how the system of reciprocity works, and because it is good for others, as well as ourselves. Most importantly, it helps us amass more positive energy and abundance so we can do even more for ourselves and everyone around us. *"Giving multiplies my ability to keep giving."*

When we find ourselves in ego to ego warfare with someone, we do have a choice whether we want to stay at war or rise above. Realize: *"The moment I choose to see the soulfulness in others, I will have already brought out the soulfulness in me."*

We will always reap what we sow, so if we share the best of ourselves today, we can expect some goodness to come back to us tomorrow. *"Mindful of what part of myself I am choosing to share."*

*A*gonizing or complaining about where we are in our lives will keep us stuck exactly where we don't want to be in our lives! Acceptance and appreciation of where we are now and how far we have already come—now that will prompt forward movement! Aspire to go further; have the willingness to do what it takes. Each morning, repeat: *"I'm stepping into my life on purpose today, willing to be the best I can be!"*

*S*ometimes we become weakened by what we hear, see, and feel coming from the outside world. We need to keep in mind that the love we are able to generate from our hearts is more powerful than any external negativity we are subjected to. When we feel our human self start to fall, we just have to say, *"I rise to the power of love."*

*O*ur Souls want us to be in a now-time zone because if we spend even one moment agonizing over yesterday or anxious about tomorrow, it is a sign there is no connection to the moment, our higher self, or Higher Power. *"Stay present in the present."*

*W*hining is a symptom of disempowerment; a notion that we have no control. The only way to go from whiner to winner is to realize there is always something we can do to create positive change. Whether we rise to the call, accept things as they are, or change our perception of all of it... we need to remember that *"Empowerment is a choice."*

*H*appiness is a decision, and each second we live and breathe, we are just one decision away from feeling the happiest we can possibly feel in that moment. Choose what is appropriate and repeat: *"Inhaling happiness in; exhaling sadness out. Inhaling happiness in; exhaling sorrow out. Inhaling happiness in; exhaling regret out. Inhaling happiness in; exhaling unforgiveness out. Inhaling and exhaling happiness!"*

*W*e should not give up on ourselves. Never, ever give up! No matter what shape we find ourselves in physically, emotionally, or mentally, we can choose to lift higher and see beyond what our ego selves have gotten us into. There is always another way to think, another direction to take, and another emotion we can fill our hearts with. Choose to *"Hear, see, and feel all the greatness that exists within me."*

$\mathcal{M}$y dear Soul Child, I'm sitting with you today to let you know things may get rough for you in the years to come. You may not feel loved all the time; you might actually be hurt by people who are supposed to protect you, and you will experience many tearful days because you don't understand others' motives. I want you to know, right now, all of this will make you stronger! You will overcome; you will grow up to be an amazing and awesome adult *because* of what you came through. When you feel alone and unsure of tomorrow, remember you are loved, you are special, and most importantly, you are powerful enough to soar above all that life has in store for you. You are like an eagle, little one, and

"Where you are going, only eagles fly!"

$\mathcal{T}$here is no reason to live 'simply human' when we can choose to live soulfully blessed. When woefulness sets in, bring the soulfulness out! Repeat: *"I feel gratitude for all I have, all that is coming in, and all there is for me in this lifetime."*

$\mathcal{S}$ometimes it is essential to move toward resistance as that will lead us to the blocks that are holding us in abeyance. In order to get back into the right flow, we should initially go against the current and take a strong stance with any part of ourselves that is in denial or fear. *"Lovingly but firmly pushing myself through this."*

$\mathcal{A}$bsolutely, we can change our perception of a hurtful and traumatic past! We can go back in time and rewrite how we want to perceive it, feel about it, and deal with it. Whether we label a painful episode as sorrowful or empowering, crushing or uplifting, damaging or helpful, it is our choice how we interpret, internalize, and categorize our life events. *"I'm choosing to see the value in every life experience."*

Our past will eventually catch up with us; we can't keep running from it. When we feel overwhelmed by the thought of going back to face it, we should remain right where we are, then stand tall like a tree and allow all our painful, remorseful, and scary memories to fall from us like dead leaves. Doing so will prepare us for the next season of new growth. Repeat this powerful mantra written by Saint Francis de Sales: ***"Blooming right where I'm planted."***

a consistently negative attitude can really stink up the place! It is as if we are sitting in a dirty diaper and alienating everyone we come in contact with. Unfortunately, while in that predicament, we tend to remain oblivious to the offensive energy emanating from our being and how it is affecting our loved ones, friends, co-workers, and everyone else we come in contact with. The only way to check our own dirty diaper is to look, listen, and be honest with ourselves about other people's reactions to our behavior and verbiage. It is our prerogative to stay unchanged and reeking from negativity, or we can opt at any given moment, for a clean, fresh start. How we present ourselves to the world is always our choice. ***"Emanating love and joy today."***

$\mathcal{T}$ime will tell but only if we ask it to! Playing wait-and-see or show-and-seek… it's always our choice how long we are willing to wait for time. *"I'm ready, willing, and able to take the next step!"*

$\mathcal{W}$e are human and may occasionally be in doubt of what we are doing to hold ourselves back, but that's okay! As long as we keep listening in our right ear to the promptings of our Souls, we will reach our lofty goals. Tell the very human self, *"Everything is as it should be; everything is going to be all right."*

$\mathcal{R}$eminder: *"If I keep hoping 'things' will get better tomorrow, I won't be concentrating on how good I can make 'things' today!"*

$\mathcal{I}$t is our choice to live in the mundane or to recognize greatness in ourselves; to stay down and repressed or tap into the potential we have to live life fully. We need to *will* a positive and empowering attitude, and NOW is always the perfect time to do so. *"I have gifts, and I'm using them."*

$\mathcal{W}$hen anger and frustration make us want to speak our minds, we should try another approach: *"Speak my heart."*

*O*ur thoughts carry influential power and, for better or for worse, they have the ability to prompt tremendous change. So if we want our thoughts to help and not hurt our circumstances, we have to take control of them. ***"Positive thoughts lead to an empowered life."***

*T*rying to run away from the truth will just keep it chasing after us. Asking for the truth to be revealed and then being brave enough to hear, see, and deal with it—that is the only way to successfully walk into our future. ***"Nothing can propel me faster than truth and willingness."***

*N*ote to My Ego Self: Why are you expecting people to be like you, to think like you, or to act like you? Get over yourself! No one is like you, and ***"Everyone is allowed to be different!"***

*I*t will be hard to spread goodness outside of ourselves if we are not filling up with goodness on the inside. Choose all day long to ***"Eat well; breathe deeply; think positive."***

When we think we are failing or not reaching our full potential, we need to remember that our life journey offers us daily opportunities to rise. Let's consider each day to be our challenge—a way to utilize our innate gifts, talents, and power, and to literally bring out the best in ourselves and what our humanness has to offer. Repeat: *"I love discovering ways to be better at being Me!"*

Love and forgiveness should be our preferred 'weapons' against our own anger. Any negative tactic we use as revenge will return more negativity and cause more pain. Instead, try *"Bringing forth love and positive gain!"*

Deciding to live a no-fault life means we can no longer lay blame on anyone or anything. Instead, when experiencing a crisis, some drama, or an uncomfortable situation, we can ask ourselves, "What is my participation, my truth, and the human lesson I am learning?" Then we should start *"Walking forward, stronger and more powerful for knowing all of it."*

When we decide to let unconditional love flow out from our hearts toward another, irrespective of any negative emotion they are trying to push toward us, we create powerful energy around ourselves that acts as a "Spiritual Order of Protection." Nothing is stronger; nothing can get past, around, or through it because *"Nothing can undermine the energy of love."*

While experiencing an uncomfortable situation, thought, or feeling, we need to hold onto the belief that everything can turn out for the best. Being uncomfortable gives us the chance to examine what we need to change, move away from, or heal. All perceived negativity affords us the opportunity to form a better understanding and a more positive outlook. *"This is my opportunity to grow."*

If we stay on the path of right and good, we will not only survive difficult life circumstances, we will help ourselves and everyone around us to thrive through them. *"Integrity Road leads to strength, power, and success."*

We each have 37 trillion cells in our bodies—give or take a few hundred million—and they all resonate every second with what is on our minds and in our hearts. So today, spend time *"SuperCharging every cell with positive power!"*

Understand that we can't be loving and raging at the same time. It is energetically impossible to bring love into our hearts when severe anger still exists inside. Decide to glean the truth about negative emotions and then let them go. *"Making room for love."*

We have to leave our pasts in the past, but before we leave them behind, let's take the wisdom gained with us. Realistically, lessons will learn new ways to catch up with us when we don't learn from them. *"Learning, healing, and growing."*

No person, place, or thing we perceive as negative will have a negative effect on us unless we allow it to. We can choose to break down tough life episodes into realizations, reminders, lessons, and clues, so new paths that highlight our greatest and highest good can be revealed. *"Maintaining positive forward movement."*

No matter what our human/ego selves keep telling us and no matter what unsettling emotions we think we need to keep, there is only one truth we need to hold onto: When we forgive another, the only thing we lose is *un*forgiveness; everything else is a gain.

"I choose empowerment;
I choose love."

If we are whining, we aren't standing in our true light, and that is not how we should appear to the world every day. *"Standing in power; walking with purpose; shining my light."*

The human body is durable but not invincible, and it is important that we love ourselves enough to take care of the amazing vessels we came here with. Remaining emotionally healthy is also important so each cell in our body will be able to resonate at its most loving and powerful frequency. Repeat: *"I respect, honor, and care for the body that carries me."*

It takes so much more energy to be anxious than it does to be calm. Feeling anything less than positive about our current state of affairs will chip away at our position of power. Have faith that *"All is and will be right and good."*

Souls are limitless and powerful. They know no boundaries, so why would we ever allow our human ego to impose any? Live *"Boundless and free."*

We must investigate before we propagate! Thoughts and opinions that consistently come into our heads should be explored and properly manipulated into worthwhile ideas before we allow them to multiply and affect our future emotions, actions, direction, health, and wellness. *"Thinking worthy thoughts today!"*

We can't help someone who isn't willing to help themselves. It is like trying to fill up a bucket with a hole in it, and leaky buckets never get filled. Instead of depleting ourselves by helping those who refuse to help themselves or pushing people who don't want to move forward, we can love everyone as they are; pray for them; be the example they can follow, and possibly help them with words of encouragement. When we focus our forward-moving energy on worthwhile endeavors, we produce even more goodness and power for ourselves and others. It is our right to help people, but we may need to ask ourselves, *"Is helping this person the right thing to do?"*

Happiness is a choice! We can choose to enjoy this day. We have permission to enjoy this day. We can *"Find and feel the joy in this day!"*

$\mathcal{N}$o matter how far from goodness a person seems to be, when we look for the good in them through loving eyes, we will raise them up. We need to remember that sometimes the only way some people will be able to tap into the goodness of their own Soul is by seeing and feeling it through ours. *"Going Soul searching today!"*

$\mathcal{I}$ntegrity is not an elusive virtue; it is either within us and recognizable to others, or it is not. It is not occasional; we are either trustworthy and accountable, or we are not. It is always our decision how we conduct ourselves, so considering we will get back everything that we put out, it makes sense to *"Put integrity into everything said and done today."*

$\mathcal{P}$ositive Manipulation® gives us the ability to change each facet of our human persona. It demands of us to lovingly let go of any negative ego commentary in favor of the beautiful promptings of our Souls. If we don't like what our minds are saying to us; we can manipulate them! Don't like the condition our bodies are in; manipulate on behalf of them! Don't like the emotions we are feeling; manipulate out of them! Why settle on simply human when we can be *"Sublimely soulful."*

When we are thinking and acting through ego; when we are only calling on our 'simply human' traits, education, and belief systems; when we feel fear, anxiety, or anger that takes us out of a loving state of being, then we have forgotten an important part of ourselves. That is okay, though; after all, we are human, but we never have to limit ourselves that way. We can choose to recognize any simply human, limited state of being as a sign that we need help remembering who we really are and what we are capable of. There is always Higher Knowing—a vibration, feeling, and resonation—we can rise to. So when in need, repeat: ***"Tapping into the power available to me, right here and right now!"***

We need to be legends in our own minds! We need to get clear in our heads about our goals by envisioning ourselves as whoever we want to become. After all, where else can we be whatever and whoever we want without interference from the rest of the world? Let's release the hold any doubt has placed on our potential by repeating: ***"I am a walking, talking billboard of my dreams and aspirations."***

ℰven with all our recent scientific advancements, we still haven't revealed all the secrets that the human body, mind, and Soul carry. Scientific minds still don't fully understand our ability to communicate with each other without words, nor do they fully comprehend the amazing and powerful relationship between our human brains and hearts. We have no clue how potent our prayer and healing potential are but, lucky for us, we don't have to wait for more to be discovered before we can utilize any of it! We can benefit from our spiritual gifts right now, every day, and every minute we want to. Think about this… before gravity was defined, we were still using it. No one was floating off the ground back then because science didn't understand physics! And the same can be said for the energy behind prayer, meditation, and the power that love, goodness, compassion, gratitude, tolerance, and forgiveness carry. So believe and have faith and trust in the omnipotent force we were created with. When more of us do this, we will all see profound results. ***"The more I believe in myself and the powers that be, the more the whole world can receive from me."***

No matter what human state someone resides in, we need to remember they were once a child—perfect, innocent, beaming with purity, and untouched by life. As we hold onto this perfection in this person, we pave the way for their true essence and authentic self to emerge. Unconditional understanding is a powerful tool, which, not only helps others shine, it helps us shine as well. *"Encourage and allow."*

The "woe-is-me" mentality just brings in more things to feel woeful about. It is easier to take responsibility for what goes on in our lives because, once we do, we can take control. Once we take control, we will be able to create positive change. *"Being in charge of my mind puts me in more power of my destiny!"*

The second we decide to change our minds—to go inward and *Positively Manipulate®* our negative thoughts into positive—all the molecules in our bodies will change with them. Recite: *"Think good; feel good."*

*E*instein said that time might actually be standing still, and we are the ones who are moving forward through time. So let's create our new reality by imagining ourselves stepping out of bed each morning moving through each day in the direction we want to go. We will walk through doors that open to our most profound opportunities; we will take the paths which lead us toward our most abundant resources; we will run into the amazing people and things we have been asking for—all while holding onto this thought: *"Time isn't passing me by; I am passing through time."*

*D*uring any moment of any day, we can visualize a force field of powerful energy emanating from our heart and acting as a shield. Then we can walk forward in confidence believing in the shield's ability to protect us from unwanted and unsolicited energy. No matter how much someone tries to block or push us, or how much we may deviate from our altruistic goals and positive state of being, we will be soulfully protected and brought right back on track once we command this protection for ourselves. *"Moving through today feeling safe and at peace."*

$\mathcal{I}$f we want to live a purpose-driven life, we have to demand it of ourselves each and every day. As we get out of bed and place our feet on the ground, we need to speak our intention: *"I'm **stepping into my day on purpose, ready, willing, and able to co-create the life I am meant to lead; the life that will bring happiness, wellness, and prosperity to myself and everyone around me!"***

$\mathcal{T}$here is never a better *time* than the present to allow *time* to work for us. Let's be mindful of our minutes, whether they are spent working, exercising, envisioning, meditating, praying, reading, or just resting and rejuvenating, because each one is an opportunity to improve our state of being. Growing older today or growing better… it's always our choice. *"Making every minute count."*

$\mathcal{N}$o if, and, or but today! Let's start moving forward with a fearless attitude, and let's also be super excited to see just how far this is going to take us. *"Fearless and mighty!"*

$\mathcal{W}$e can be victims of circumstance or victors over circumstance; it is always our choice. This decision should be a no-brainer, because the second we put the victim mentality on hold, we allow for our victorious self to dictate all future directions we take. What a difference positive talk creates. *"Bold and victorious!"*

$\mathcal{P}$ositive Manipulation® is a simple process that allows us to put our human ego on a break while we give our more soulful side a chance to show and tell us a better way to be. *"I'm ready to listen to my better half."*

$\mathcal{I}$f we keep claiming that others are treating us badly, we might miss out on opportunities to heal our own personas. Other people's actions toward us and reactions to us might actually offer an indication of our own level of self-esteem (what we feel about our selves), and the quality of the energy we may be sitting in and exuding out (what is going on in our subconscious). So if we consistently experience the same negative reaction from various people, there may be some truth about ourselves we need to see and hear. Acknowledge that *"Everyone has the potential to be my messenger."*

When our self-image, esteem, and worthiness are not up to a high standard and we see ourselves in a negative light, it will be difficult for others to see us any differently. Realistically, we cannot expect someone else to love and honor us more than we are willing to love and honor ourselves. *"Allowing for a new and powerful self-image."*

When we decide to see the goodness, power, and light in someone, the goodness, power, and light will be shown. *"Seeking the Soul."*

Understand that it is possible to physically leave someone who has deceived or hurt us in some way, and still love them more *heartfully* and spiritually. We can still believe in the beauty of their Soul and at the same time, recognize their current human state of mind and body as something we don't want to be around. *"Disconnecting from what is no longer necessary; holding onto all that is right and good."*

Don't give up on love; give into it! When we find ourselves in an argument with a loved one, instead of going into self-protection mode, we can use love to put a "Spiritual Order of Protection" on the relationship. Rather than pulling apart and dividing to conquer each other, we can pull together and conquer the issue! By offering love, we will realize the best of what the relationship has to offer. *"Giving into Love."*

There will be a time when someone's verbiage makes us feel truly uncomfortable. When this happens, we can walk away, or we can ask ourselves if this is what we need to hear in order to grow forward. Words don't have to harm us. They aren't bullets that can penetrate our skin; they are not knives that cut. They might actually be the answer to our question and/or prayer request, but we would need to make the decision to listen with our hearts before our heads make a quick judgment. That decreases the impact the words have on our persona as it opens our minds to the wisdom that might be coming through. *"Be open to hearing what needs to be said."*

The most powerful insult any one of us usually has to handle in a day is from our own mind, not from another's mouth! *"Making all my self-talk into motivational magic."*

Science has proven that our emotional energy will radiate from our bodies and connect with everyone we come in contact with. To make that energy feel good to others, we need to decide to make it good! Imagine that a 'heartlight' exists inside our chests that can be turned on with the flip of a switch… a mental switch, that is. Today, go for the glow! Try to overwhelm people with good intentions. *"Turn on my heartlight."*

It is true that misery loves company but only *"Happiness attracts the fun crowd."*

Gainful truth, that which will help us move forward successfully, is always available to us, but sometimes our hearts and minds will reject our intuition. Knowing might mean we will have to do something we are not ready to do, or perhaps it will force us to see what we haven't been able to face. To move forward successfully, we would have to be willing to push past all fear and denial and be ready to see, hear, and feel what our intuition already knows. As soon as a state of willingness and readiness is reached, we will have the ability to access truth, knowledge, and any insights that are available. After full disclosure, we can still choose to stay right where we are, but it will be because we want to, not because we are too afraid to know. ***"Growing forward in truth."***

Wanting just multiplies the wanting; lack multiplies the lack. Gratitude also multiplies itself so the more grateful we are for what we have, the more we will walk into things to be grateful for. ***"Keeping an attitude of gratitude."***

α note from me, your Soul: Some people believe that forgiveness has rules; that there are crimes against the body and heart that warrant a lifetime of anger and hatred. From a human standpoint, that may be true, but together we are more than human. Believe that forgiveness, just like love, has no boundaries that aren't imposed. There is never a good reason not to forgive; there is just unwillingness! It is your prerogative to live with *un*forgiveness, but that would mean you would be living in obedience to it and in pain and anger from it. These are emotions that grip the throat and harden the heart. I don't want this to affect your life and happiness forever, and whether they deserve forgiveness or not, *we* do! Choose forgiveness, happiness, wholeness, and love because everyone around us deserves to enjoy the best of who we are. Become unchained from what happened back then so it will never, ever affect you again.

"Choosing forgiveness means choosing freedom."

What we are in denial of might actually be the most important piece of information we can use to grow forward harmonically. Perhaps we initially go into denial for good reason, but that doesn't mean there isn't an even better reason to come out of it! Choose to uncover whatever it is that is too maddening, frightening, or hurtful to face. *"Ready, willing, and able to see and hear all I need to grow forward in strength and love."*

Arrogance is a state of mind, while confidence is a state of knowing. Arrogance is a learned trait; confidence is an earned trait. Arrogance blocks our potential, but confidence is the building block for potential. Arrogance breeds insolence, while confidence breeds self-assurance. Arrogance creates boundaries, but confidence pushes us through them. We need to remain in a state of confidence knowing that no amount of arrogance will ever take us where we want to go. *"Gifted by Grace."*

Perfect Love exists, but it needs to be activated. By placing the sanctity and health of our love relationship in higher regard than our human need to self-protect and defend, we can begin to achieve perfection in that relationship. To start, both partners need to strive for unconditional love for both the Soul and human aspects of each other. Then a commitment must be made to change individual wants and needs into what is needed, wanted, as well as right and good for the whole. When each partner does this, neither will ever feel a deficit because the relationship will become greater and more powerful than the sum of its two parts. For Perfect Love to become a reality, two must unite for the single purpose of trying to be better together than they are apart. *"Perfect Love will right the wrongs in imperfect people."*

We can feel momentarily devastated to find out someone lied to us and still be grateful when the truth is finally revealed. After all, living a life surrounded by lies is never better than living a life rooted in truth. *"Living stronger because of it."*

They say when two souls are ready to come together for a higher purpose, that nothing—no distance or circumstance—can keep them apart. So, in order to walk into whoever we are supposed to meet, we need to state and believe: *"All paths leading to my Soul connections are clear."*

We need to maintain a peaceful state of being so everyone feeling our energy today will benefit. Instead of pushing negative emotions out toward others, we need to go inward and use loving thoughts to manipulate what we think and feel that keeps us imbalanced and restless. This makes the influence we have on everyone as positive as it can be. *"Radiating Peace."*

We are co-creators but how can the other half of our creation team start working if we don't first initiate the process? We need to dream big today… to think about and *feel* positively charged about what we can achieve. And finally, we need to see ourselves living our best life because all of what we are capable of will only become apparent *after* we know it, not before. *"Today my potential becomes my reality."*

The moment we realize how exhausted we are from trying so hard, we should become aware that we are "muscling it" by trying to resolve an issue or complete a task the human way. Our human strength and intellect, though—that's not our true source of power! We are at our most profound state of being when we stop trying to muscle it our way and allow for soulful inspiration to take over.

*"Human self, step back and relax.
I'm flexing my spiritual muscles now."*

Happiness is not an emotion that stems from the material world; it is not a concept we were taught. We were all born with the ability to be and stay happy with very little. Happiness would have to be an intrinsic part of our being, or we wouldn't know what it feels like to be unhappy! This knowingness should make us want to stop looking on the outside for what already exists on the inside. *"Happiness is always there for the asking."*

What would this day be like if we started acknowledging our courage instead of our sorrows? Let's find out! *"Making all woes into wows!"*

We need to remember that when we think about what we don't have, we are existing in the energy of lack. When we obsess over what we want, we are perpetuating a lack of faith and disbelief in our ability to achieve and acquire. Only thoughts and feelings of gratitude and abundance will help us bring about all that we are willing to strive for. *"Grateful for all I have now and for all that is coming to me."*

We can control many aspects of our own lives, but we cannot control another's. Even if we see what the other person is doing to hurt themselves and we know and want to help them see a better way, we cannot force them to listen. Instead of being helpful, it will seem pushy; it may feel offensive and scary. It might actually be *our* way and not necessarily *their* best way. After all, they may need to turn down a few wrong roads in order to realize the right ones. On the contrary, though, when someone is truly ready, willing, and able to move forward and do whatever it takes to help themselves, everything we offer—the exchange of energy, help, advice, and love —will come easy and bring empowerment to ourselves and to them! Until then, though, we should love them unconditionally, be an example they can follow, and leave ourselves available to aide and guide those who really are ready and able to accept what we are willing to give. Our daily, self-reminder: *"Why push when all I really need to do is lead?"*

When negative commentary flies at us, we can choose to evade it, block it, counter it, or take the hit. As we grow in awareness of the power of love, we realize that evasion might seem appropriate sometimes, but it won't rectify a situation. A block might help us, but it may not stop the other person from coming at us again. A counter will only instigate more of the same, and a hit from their ego to ours could go on forever! So love really is our greatest form of protection. Every day that we make the choice to wear it like a shield, we willfully go into our life episodes with the knowingness that we are *"Protected and ready for anything."*

a plea to my Soul: "Can I do this today... Can I believe I am boundless and that nothing can keep me from what I want to accomplish; that my past won't hold me back; and that I can be what I want to be now irrespective of what happened to me back then? Can I let go of any doubt that I possess the power to make my life amazing?" And the Soul Self replies, "Uh, YEAH! And if believing in yourself doesn't work for you by the end of today, you have my permission to go back to being doubtful tomorrow." *"I believe in Me."*

Nothing said and done today will have a negative effect on us unless we allow it to. We have the option of deflecting what is not useful while at the same time *"Gleaning and holding onto everything worthwhile."*

Anger is not a good defense against further damage or pain someone can inflict on us. It is an energy that is more useful and powerful after we manipulate it into an action of love that will help us achieve positive gain. And when we stop to think about it, most of our anger is at ourselves for allowing others to take advantage of us. We can learn from that. We can honor our own space, time, and life and remember that *"Honoring myself changes every outcome."*

We shouldn't be angry at others for 'triggering' our emotions. In fact, we should be soulfully thanking people who trigger us! Our emotional triggers are our clues to what is holding us in abeyance and preventing us from utilizing our innate spiritual gifts and potential. *"Recognize; heal; release."*

𝒫erception, it can be said, is 9/10's the law; meaning that the wrongful opinions other people hold of us may belong to them, but they still create a reality *we* may have to deal with. Since everyone perceives at their own level of understanding, we could try to give the person the benefit of the doubt. We could choose to ignore their comments, walk away, or discontinue our relationship with them. We could also rectify an untruth orally, in writing, or by using Soul-to-Soul Communication. We can even pray or meditate for more truth to be revealed by asking ourselves, "Is there any validity in what this person is saying?" Irrespective of what we choose to do, we should always have gratitude for the opportunity to learn and grow from what we may not have seen on our own. *"I appreciate all I am being shown."*

𝒪ld age will have its rewards, but only if we allow bad habits to die young. Repeat: *"Letting go of what no longer serves me."*

ote to my Ego Self: I'm gathering up what no longer serves us and letting it all go. Since I want to travel far on this road to wellness, it makes sense to get rid of our heavy load. I'm expecting us to be carrying less and less with each step we take, every day and all along the way. So, start helping me

"Lighten up!"

Gratitude never has to translate into complacency! Being happy with what we have today does not preclude us from bringing in even more to be happy about tomorrow. So acknowledge the fact that *"Being grateful brings in more to be grateful for."*

Positive feelings—our positive thoughts combined with our loving emotions—create 'coherent rhythms' which radiate outside of our bodies into what scientists call "The Field." Unloving emotions create incoherent rhythms. So when we are radiating something negative and unhealthy, we will feel and experience more discord. When we are radiating something positive and good, we will feel and experience more peace and love. We can control the energy we exude out into the field by creating an intention to be *"Positive, loving, and coherent."*

When our minds are full of history and regret, there is no room for inspiration, joy, and success! We need to empty out the old and stale to allow for the new and unveiled. Today start *"Clearing space to showcase my beautiful visions."*

Who is the common denominator in all of our life episodes? The answer we hear in our heads should always be a resounding, "Me!" And that discovery should comfort us because if we can find the source of our issues within ourselves, then we can do something about it, which will change all our circumstances going forward. Why make ourselves into a victim by laying fault and blame when we can *"Accept responsibility and move forward in awareness and power."*

Profound advancement can only occur when we change all our 'what ifs' into 'why not!' *"Taking the steps necessary to make these dreams become my reality."*

We cannot start with "I hate my … " and expect to easily get to "I love my … !" If we want to attract the good stuff, we need to look for the good in the stuff we already have. Body, living arrangements, career, relationships, family, friends… *"Loving and appreciating all I have right here, right now."*

$\mathcal{P}$eace does have a price, and it's called "Surrender." When we are existing in a state of turmoil and everything we do is still not enough, we need to put our troubles "up". Whether it is a Higher Power we send them to or our own Higher Knowing, we never have to work hard at bringing Love and Grace into a situation. *"Surrendering to All Things Good."*

$\mathcal{I}$f people label us as 'too weak,' we should ask ourselves if we are too needy. Neediness creates a 'pulling' energy that seeks to draw people in, making them feel exhausted. We shouldn't be relying on anyone to do what we ought to be doing for ourselves, either. On the other hand, if we are consistently being called out for being too strong because we are so demanding, our question should then be, "Am I expecting too much from everyone? Is my energy 'pushing' them?" In every person's opinion of us, there may be some important information we can use to advance on our wellness journey. When we decide to look for the truth in all our interactions with others, we show respect for what they are thinking and feeling, as well as bringing honor to our own process of self-growth. *"Listening with openness and readiness."*

Woe is me or *whoa*, it's me?—One mindset will bring more woe; the other gets us out of drama every single time. When we become brave enough to look at ourselves in the mirror and ask this question, everything we reflect going forward will change. *"Taking responsibility for the direction my life is taking."*

$a$gonizing over what went on yesterday or getting anxious about what might happen tomorrow will not allow us to connect with the part of ourselves that wants us to be in this moment creating, enjoying, sharing, loving and giving. Spend today's moments *"Living in now-time."*

9f we want a great job, we have to commit to being a great employee. If we want a true friend we can count on, we have to be a true friend someone can count on. If we want a wonderful partner to share our life with, then we have to be a wonderful partner someone would want to share their life with! Remember: *"I'm worthy of getting back exactly what I am willing to give."*

A New Day Acknowledgement

I am **inspired** by a higher knowing within me, and I am mentally challenging myself to transcend any negative (ego) tendencies, needs, and wants to do what is right and good for the whole.

I am **aspiring** from within my heart to love unconditionally and boundlessly with ultimate forgiveness.

I am **motivated** from deep within my gut to constantly and consistently strive to be the best human being I can possibly be.

With Inspiration, Aspiration,
and Motivation,
"I am Soul Power personified!"

α negative mindset is such a turn-off! It turns off our creative process, our positive flow of internal and external energy, and our ability to hear and see solutions. It also turns off any potential we might have to render positive change, and it diminishes our capacity to attract anything better than what we are thinking at that moment. Essentially, a negative mindset leaves us without power, and why would we want to remain powerless, close-minded, and in the dark, when we actually possess so much inherent power, genius, and light? It's just a flip of our mental switch, so today, let's choose to *"Flip over to power!"*

$\mathfrak{I}$t makes sense that we would need to love some aspect of our current job to move onto a better one, or to love our physical state of being as it is, even if we want to change it. We would have to glean goodness from our current relationships to attract more goodness going forward. Remember this truth: if we keep reminding ourselves of what is good about our lives, we start resonating with more of what we want, and not with what we don't want. *"Seeing all there is to be happy about!"*

Until we let go of the hurt and pain from a past relationship, we may attract new relationships and partners that bring in the same drama over and over again. Since we are the common denominator in all our life-episodes, we need to take responsibility for what may be going on in our subconscious that needs to heal. We also have to recognize that any drama cycle we find ourselves in is probably a 'clear sign' that reminds us to *"Clear the past to make room for a better future!"*

It takes time because we make it take time. Forgiving, forgetting, and healing from betrayal will take as long as we let it take. Having patience with ourselves and the process of healing is good, but knowing when enough is enough is sublime! *"Helping myself move beyond this."*

Having gratitude is the fastest way to change the energy of want, need, and lack of wealth into abundance, clarity, and physical health. *"Recognizing all I have to be grateful for!"*

When we avoid people who trigger our weaknesses, we may be running away from what we need to address and heal in ourselves. Asking, hoping, or expecting other people not to trigger us is not a good idea either. That would mean we are demanding them to be healthier than we are! We should make the decision to overcome our sore spots, so in the future, we will be able to stand firm, balanced, and uninfluenced by another person's intentional or unintentional negative effect on our psyche. Choose to *"Confront and then heal from triggers."*

When we feel the anger monger start to rise in us, we need to become warriors! It is time to don our shields of love and wield our swords of truth so we can conquer that negativity...not in others but in ourselves. *"Love can conquer this!"*

The field of energy that surrounds us is like a bank, and we each have a preferred account. Whatever good we do will create a deposit, and whenever we are in need, we will be offered a withdrawal. The more good we do for the sake of the whole, the more interest and dividends are applied. So today, find ways to *"Engage in random acts of goodness."*

$\mathcal{S}$tay a victim or strive to be a victor ...? It is always our choice. ***"I am victorious!"***

$\mathcal{W}$hen we start tallying up and recalling all that we have to be thankful for, the complaining side of our brains will shut down and the power of gratitude will start lifting up our hearts. And that state of mind and heart is synonymous with happiness. Today, make the choice to ***"Tally up!"***

$\mathcal{T}$here will always be people we encounter who want to push our buttons and bring us down to the same level of humanness they are at, but we don't have to go to that level with them. If we decide to stay engaged with our Soul, we never have to worry about 'falling' from their grace. Realistically, no one can knock us down without our permission. ***"Standing strong and soulful."***

$\mathcal{O}$ur intuition is our greatest strength, and whatever there is in this universe that isn't explainable —that is where Soul lives! It is important for us to trust more in what is not physically seen and audibly heard because when we do, the best part of who we are will be realized. ***"Trusting the small voice."***

$\mathcal{M}$edical science has been proving that meditating on a health issue with thankfulness and belief in our ability to heal from it will bring our ailing body back to balance. So that means that a gratitude a day will keep the doctor away! Today, no matter what shape we think we are in, we need to believe we are: *"Healing and restoring."*

$\mathcal{C}$onsidering we won't get it back again, we should take full advantage of this day. Let's keep pushing beyond distractions and discomfort so we can take utilize of all this time we have been granted. *"Achieving all my wellness goals."*

$\mathcal{I}$t can be said that it is harder to stay in woe and heartache than it is to get oneself out. Anytime we attempt to emotionally rise up, we are better off than when we remain mentally down. *"Visualize the Rise!"*

$\mathcal{N}$ote to my Ego Self: I'm turning politely away from you today. It makes no sense to keep using my limited human side as a daily guide, considering *"I have a boundless Soul in whom I can rely!"*

$\mathcal{W}$e don't have to accept the status quo if we aren't happy with it. Let's make the decision today to utilize every single magnificent part of our beings to enhance every single aspect of our lives. Repeat: ***"The process of change begins with me!"***

$\mathcal{P}$ositive Manipulation® is the key to mental freedom. Say, "No, not good enough!" to any negative mindset; to whatever is not working for the higher good; to what doesn't feel positive and loving, and to what does not bring wholeness and understanding. ***"Saying YES to all that is good."***

$\mathcal{I}$t is normal to go into self-protection mode when we argue with a loved one, but that habit will pull us apart from one another. Why divide and defend when we can instead unite and resolve? Choose to stand with conviction in the knowledge that ***"There is no issue too big that love can't make small."***

$\mathcal{R}$eminder to my Ego: ***"The more you blame, the more things stay the same; the more you whine, the less you shine!"***

ℐf we stop to think about it, there were occasions in our lives—even if they were just fleeting moments—when we felt good. Perhaps our bills got paid and there was money left over; at least one person loved us unconditionally, and we were able to do things that made us happy. Maybe there were times when we were so strong, we thought we could conquer the world. Realistically, all sorts of positive memories and emotions are there for us to call upon when we need them. They are as available to us as the negative nonsense that often finds its way into our heads. So if we want to create and maintain health, wealth, and everything wonderful, we have to replace negative mental dialogue with fresh ideas and thoughts of gratitude, abundance, love, and joy. And if we need a jumpstart, we have all those amazing memories to call upon. *"Remembering the joy, peace, and love in my life."*

Through forgiveness and unconditional love, we can rewrite the past, restore our energy, renegotiate some boundaries, and remaster a negative mental state. All this, so we don't have to relive or rehash a whole lot of stuff we should be leaving behind! *"Forgiveness is the key to my restoration."*

If we all eventually reap what we sow, why would we choose to sow what we don't want to reap? Today, we can do, say, and act toward others the way we want others to do, say, and act toward us. *"Planting seeds that yield worthwhile outcomes."*

The power that created us never left us. It is running through every cell in our bodies every second of every day, allowing our hearts to beat and our blood to flow. While here, we don't have to worry about not having this life-giving energy at our disposal. It is always there just waiting to be recognized and utilized. *"Tapping into life force!"*

Our inside dialogue is more important to our health, well being, relationships, and success than anything else we hear on the outside. And the best part about that: we have control over what is being said on the inside! *"My thoughts empower me."*

Walk forward today with a big set... mindset that is! Repeat: *"I am the real deal; I am realizing my goals!"*

Lowering our expectations of what others can or will do for us will yield high rewards. The truth is when we rely on people to take care of our needs, we halt our own co-creating potential, which hinders our ability to take care of ourselves. We also create an energy of need that makes others feel they pushed or pulled. Instead of putting our expectations out toward others, we can put them up; up to our Higher Knowing and Power. We need to realize that people can barely get their own needs met, so why would we expect them to properly take care of ours? Repeat: *"Putting my expectations up and expecting my needs to be met."*

When our minds are full of history, regrets, what ifs, and judgments, there is no room for creative genius! We need to empty out the old, stale, can't-get-me-anywhere thoughts and *"Allow for genius to flow."*

It is good to realize, appreciate, and understand feelings of righteous indignation, but if we allow that emotion to form our opinions without adding love and compassion, the opinions may come off as ridicule, anger, and judgment. To bring love into all our conversations, we must strive to be *"Pure of Heart."*

When we listen to gossip or judgmental opinion about someone, we will be co-mingling with the gossiping person's energy. If that energy is not in alignment with what is right and good for all—if it is not rooted in truth and love—we need to ask ourselves "Is this the energy I want resonating with every cell in my body? Is this an act I want to be duplicated in my life?" It is important for us to remember that politely walking away or changing the subject will not only help ourselves and the person being gossiped about, it will also help the person who is doing the gossiping. *"Perpetuating positive energy."*

Let us be tolerant and allow people to be who and what they need to be. If they reciprocate that tolerance, then great! If they don't, it doesn't matter. To get where we want to go, we don't need the road to tolerance to be a two-way street. *"Accept and allow."*

It doesn't take much positive energy to create a good day, but it will take an awful lot of negative energy to drag ourselves through a bad one. *"Staying inspired!"*

a note from me, your Soul: You are a special being, willing yourself to do better today than you did the day before. You may not realize this, but you are succeeding beautifully! When you think otherwise, please forgive yourself. That is a funny but often misunderstood fact about being human... You can't fail at it even when you try! So laugh at yourself often and relish in your humanness, because we would not be on this Earth without it. When you need to pick yourself up, remember you have me and the power of love and goodness inside of you. Here is the "Ho'oponopono" prayer. Repeat it often when you need to spiritually cleanse and lift: *"I'm sorry; please forgive me; I love you; thank you."*

*S*hould we spend today just getting older or doing something to become stronger, better, healthier, and smarter? Make full use of this time by *"Growing up wiser!"*

*B*e smart enough to know that no one is smart enough to know everything! Staying humble takes the onus off our limited, human brains and immediately allows for soulful wisdom to be heard. *"Happy to be humble and smarter for it!"*

We are free to say what we want, but we need to remember another "free" service here on Earth: When we judge, name call, and berate others, it brings more judgment, name calling, and berating back to us. Who can claim that they deserve any better than what they are willing to give? *"Keeping in mind the need to be kind."*

All things that seem uncomfortable or even painful can offer us something. Remember that what we decide to see as good and positive will actually become so. Ask for the truth; ask for what good exists and can come from what happened. Repeat: *"Seeing clearly now; willing my pain to become my gain."*

Sooner or later, every seed that we plant in The Field will be harvested, so if we don't stay focused on planting good seeds, we won't see any goodness growing forward. *"Planting what will bring abundance!"*

Considering we popped out of the womb in a loving state of being, it seems evident that feeling love brings us the closest we can get to our authentic selves. *"I am Love."*

There are really no right or wrong sides inasmuch as there are perceptions, opinions, provable facts, and some truth that can be gleaned from each viewpoint. Who is willing to open their minds and hearts long enough to see, hear, and discover what really exists and to appreciate another perspective other than their own? To end discord, we need to gather our opinions and perceptions, pick up our heels from where they are dug in the sand, and walk to the middle—to the "Inn Between." That's where discovery and resolution reside; in that tiny respite where there are no egos, only Souls; where wisdom will replace arrogance, and hostility, hate, anger, resentment, and *un*forgiveness can no longer take hold. The Inn Between is the place we can spend quality time basking in positive energy. And the best part about the Inn: The only cost is relinquishment; the only payment is love. ***"I am willing to see and hear more truth."***

When we look in the mirror, who and what do we see? If we can't find something we like about what is being reflected back, aren't we doing a disservice to ourselves and everyone around us? When it comes to a negative self-image, here is something to consider: ***If we can be our own worst enemy, it stands to reason we can also be our own best friend.***

"Love thyself."

We shouldn't expect people to accept us as we are if we are unhealthy and not living up to our Souls' potential. We should want to present the best of who we are so we can give ourselves the best chance of being accepted. When we do that, irrespective of the negative or positive reaction we get from others, we will still be okay within ourselves. *"When I try my best I am creating perfection in that moment."*

If the time we have here on this Earth is dependent on our bodies, then we have to make sure our bodies have everything they need to stay here for as long as we want them to stay. We can spend each day getting older or getting better; this choice is always ours to make. *"Healthy choices; healthy body; healthy life!"*

If we don't want a nasty name or label put on ourselves, we need to make it a practice not to stick one on anyone else. Calling someone out on their behavior is legitimate, but giving them the title we believe they deserve is not in our job description. Rather than labeling, *"Seek truth; remain open; listen."*

For all the IQ, education, Ph.D's, and training anyone can acquire in a lifetime, there is still no one who has discovered all there is to understand about life, or the human body and its power, potential, and energy. Why, then, would any of us live our lives relying solely on what is known to this date, when what is unknown may be more important for our growth? Today, count on the fact that there is much more to being human than we realize. Spend time dwelling in the magic and mystery of our humanness and remain open to all the soulful wisdom that reveals itself. *"Excited to discover what else there is to know!"*

We have the right to be happy or to be miserable; to decide that life is amazing or to complain about every aspect; to take in deep breaths and clean water to nourish ourselves, or to dehydrate our bodies and shallow breathe till we crash at our feet. At this moment, we can be who we came here to be, or we can excuse ourselves because of our past, our parents (or lack thereof), a job, bank account, illness, race, gender, IQ, relationship status, upbringing, and/or society. We have the right to stay exactly where we are or to *"Start walking into untapped potential!"*

$\mathcal{I}$f we keep picturing what we want, we will eventually generate the energy that goes with it. As Dr. Wayne Dyer said, "We will see it when we believe it!" Remember: *"The only 'thing' that can stand in the way of obtaining what I want is any lingering doubt that I can obtain what I want!"*

$\mathcal{S}$ociety puts so much faith and trust in evil's ability to destroy, while at the same time, so little faith and almost no trust is put in the omnipotent power and potential that love has to conquer it. Let's help flip that mentality around today! Repeat: *"Nothing can shake me out of love."*

$\mathcal{E}$very time an anxious, angry, or fearful notion finds its way into our heads, we have the option to wash over it with positive sentiments and intention. *"Pure, powerful, clean thoughts!"*

$\mathcal{W}$e can lay blame and deny, or we can exclaim and defy. We don't ever have to be victims of circumstance if we are willing to see and acknowledge our participation in all of our life episodes. Repeat: *"Taking responsibility so I can create positive change."*

No matter what negative thought process has been trying to take hold of our minds, hearts, and lives, we can decide that this day will be amazing! We can choose to rise out of what used to make us sink. We can see solutions where we used to see problems. We can glean the positive from the negative, and we can be happy for all that challenges us! Today, repeat: *"No person and no thing can stop greatness from flowing through me!"*

If we want to take credit for all that is going well today, then it makes sense that we will have to take responsibility for whatever we think is going wrong. But that shouldn't lead to anxiety because everything has a solution; everything can bring us to more awareness; everything can turn out well if we believe in our ability to *"Make all perceived 'wrongs' into rights."*

The Law of Distraction says that we will never realize what we can't visualize; we will never receive what we can't perceive, and we will never obtain a dream we can't mentally sustain. Today, we need to concentrate on what we want our life to be and then feel what it is like to already be living it. We do this until it becomes our reality. *"I see it; I feel it; it is here!"*

𝓘f we consider that every human on earth was designed as a complete package capable of obtaining everything they need and want from a completely abundant, all-inclusive universe, why then would we spend any time at all doubting our ability to achieve the life we want? When any uncertainty about our potential takes hold, we need to repeat: *"I was created in power, brought to life by power, and exist here to be power personified."*

𝓝o matter what happens during any given day, we need to remember we have our own Higher Knowing to tap into, our own Higher Power to call on, our own Souls to rely upon, and this vast System of ours to create with. Believe in the sublime knowledge that *"Even when there doesn't seem to be a way out, there is always a way to rise UP!"*

𝓦e can be our own worst enemy today or our own best friend. Embrace this knowingness! Ask: What good can come from seeing and saying only bad things about myself? Then repeat: *"There is plenty to love about Me!"*

The more willing we are to give out what we want to receive, the more our lives will become what we want them to be.

"Love boundlessly today."

My Mini Personal Index

(my favorite messages, mantras, and page numbers)

My Mini Personal Index

(my favorite messages, mantras, and page numbers)

My Mini Personal Index
(my favorite messages, mantras, and page numbers)

My Mini Personal Index

(my favorite messages, mantras, and page numbers)

About the Author

Donna Martini is a lifelong student of healthy lifestyle practices, self-healing techniques, quantum principles, and energy manipulation. She has been sharing her knowledge for over 25 years as an activist, coach, speaker, and author, through radio, video, public television, and social media. Donna dedicated her life to community service and has been helping people transcend negative emotions and thoughts, old belief systems, and physical imbalances through a technique she calls, "Positive Manipulation®." She believes we are all capable of soulful communication but would need to first "get over our human selves" in order to engage spiritually. "Our ego voice can be louder," she contends, "and we need to decide—moment to moment—who we want to listen to."

Born just two months after Hurricane Donna struck the United States in 1960, she jokingly refers to it as her earthly entry. "It's going to take a profound force," she says, "to blow through the negativity we are now experiencing in this country. I'm making it my job each day to become more loving, which will help me help others do the same." Donna believes that none of us should use the fact that we are only human as an excuse not to act "spiritually gifted." "We are more energetically powerful than we think we are," she asserts, "and we should all be using our innate gifts to help one another."

Donna maintains that she bases her life choices on the example of goodness Jesus left for us to follow. She wishes, however, to share with others what all faiths have in common while leaving religious teachings to those more capable. She feels led to help people understand their spiritual potential and she is convinced that if all of us would wake up in the morning intending to live that day trying to be better than we were the day before, the whole population would lift. She asks us, "How can we not at least try to make our world a better place for ourselves and for our children? We have been given the tools," she says, "we just have to learn how to use them." ♥

About the Mouse

MantraMouse®, as this book's mascot is affectionately named, is a reminder of how truly miniature we are in comparison to the vastness of our world and universe. Just like every creature here on Earth, the mouse has a message to offer about our ability to see each task clearly so we can take action accordingly. MantraMouse reminds us not to bypass or take for granted the seemingly small but necessary steps we need to take in order to reach our goals.

If we want to attain the big things in life, we sometimes have to stay focused on the little things. If we want to create great change in our future, we have to take some time to address the tiny details of our present moment. Small gestures can produce enormous results, and MantraMouse's daily challenges show us that we don't need to walk in fear of what is bigger than we are. Power and might exist, not in our stature, but in our minds and hearts. There should be no worries about what we can't accomplish because, in reality, there are no jobs that are too big; there's only ambition that is too small. ♥

Made in the USA
Las Vegas, NV
21 December 2020

14571363R00109